The Ultimate Venezuelan Cookbook

111 Dishes From Venezuela To Cook Right Now

Slavka Bodic

Imprint: Independently published

Please sign up for free Balkan and Mediterranean recipes:
www.balkanfood.org

Introduction

Do you want to celebrate the authentic Venezuelan flavors by cooking some delicious and savory meals at home? Then you've definitely found the right fit for you! This cookbook will introduce you to some of the most popular Venezuelan recipes and meals that you'll definitely love, especially if you've a food lover. Whether you have been to Venezuela or not, you can easily recreate its traditional cuisine at home with the help of this comprehensive cookbook. Venezuela is popular for its unique culture, languages and food and this cookbook is an easy way to come close to the flavorsome cuisine of this South American region.

The Ultimate Venezuelan cookbook will present Venezuelan cuisine and its culinary vibrant culture in a way that you may have never tried before. It brings you a variety of Venezuelan recipes in one place. The cookbook is perfect for all those who always wanted to cook Venezuelan food on their own, without the help of a native Venezuelan. Based on this Venezuelan cuisine cookbook, you can successfully create a complete Venezuelan menu, or you can try all the Venezuelan recipes on different occasions as well. In this cookbook, you'll find popular Venezuelan meals and ones that you might not have heard of formerly.

In these recipes, you'll discover some of the most commonly used Venezuelan ingredients like veggies and meats. Besides, you'll also learn how to make such ingredients and use them in different meals. The Venezuelan cuisine has been comprised of various dishes of the Venezuelan people and has been widely spread across the globe. There's a clear difference between taste and flavor in the food of various regions of Venezuela due to the differences in culture and geological locations. And in this cookbook, you'll uncover all the recipes from different parts of Venezuela.

Here's what you'll receive in this cookbook:

- Insights about Venezuelan Cuisine
- Facts About Venezuela
- Venezuelan breakfast recipes
- Appetizers
- Salads and soups
- Main Dishes
- Venezuelan desserts and drinks

Let's try all these Venezuelan Recipes and recreate a complete menu to celebrate the amazing Venezuelan flavors and unforgettable aromas!

Table of Contents

Why Venezuelan Cuisine?

Venezuelan cuisine is greatly influenced by European, Italian, Portuguese, Spanish, and French, as well as West African and Native American styles. Venezuelan food differs tremendously, depending on where you are in the country. Corn, plantains, rice, beans, yams, and a variety of meats are all staples. Within the Venezuelan diet, tomatoes, potatoes, eggplants, onions, squashes, spinach, and zucchini are all typical side dishes. Most recipes call for Aj dulce and papelón. Worcestershire sauce is frequently used in stews. Venezuela is also known for its huge range of white cheeses, which are usually named after geographical regions.

Venezuela is noted not only for its gorgeous countryside, but also for its diverse cuisine, which incorporates elements from Spanish, West African, and Native American traditions. The majority of meals are made with simple components such as corn, plantains, black beans, and meats, which give Venezuelan cuisine its distinct and delicious flavors. Even if politics and the country's current condition have recently dominated the news, there's one positive that will always be celebrated: the cuisine. In no particular sequence, below is a list of Venezuela's most famous and delectable foods.

Arepas

"There's nothing more Venezuelan than an arepa," as the popular adage goes. This corn-based "bread" is the quintessential Venezuelan cuisine, which can be served as a main course or a side dish. Arepas are unleavened corn flour patties that are flat and circular. It can be grilled, baked, or fried. Depending on the location and the cook's approach, arepas can be filled with a variety of items. They're incredibly adaptable because you may customize the dough to your liking. Some individuals like to add shredded carrots or beets to add more taste. Chia seeds, oats, and flax seeds can be used to make them healthier.

Pabellón Criollo

This is the national dish of Venezuela. Juicy pulled beef, black beans, white rice, and fried plantains make up the criollo pabellón. It's served with a slice of avocado on the side and some shredded salty white cheddar grated over the black beans. It's a flavor marriage made in heaven. The salty flavor of the beef and beans contrasts beautifully with the sweet flavor of the plantains and white rice, creating a taste sensation. There are various variations on this platter, but some claim that the sofrito of the beef is the key to any superb pabellon. The beef is cooked in a mixture of onions, sweet peppers, bell peppers, and adobo seasoning.

Tequeños

They aren't typically mozzarella sticks; in fact, they're far superior. These are fried or baked cheese sticks created with a pastry crust wrapped around salty white cheese. They're usually served with various dipping sauces, the most famous of which are guasacaca, a Venezuelan avocado-based sauce.

Venezuela

Venezuela, formally the Bolivarian Republic of Venezuela, is a country on South America's northern coast that consists of a continental landmass and several Caribbean islands and islets. Venezuela has a land area of 353,841 sq. miles (916,445 km^2), and its population was almost 29 million in 2021. Caracas is the country's capital and largest urban agglomeration. The Caribbean Sea and the Atlantic Ocean border the continental territory on the north, Colombia on the west, Brazil on the south, Trinidad and Tobago on the north-east, and Guyana on the east.

Guyana Esequiba is a claim that the Venezuelan government has against Guyana. Venezuela is a federal presidential republic with 23 states, a capital district, and federal dependencies covering the country's offshore islands. Venezuela is one of Latin America's most urbanized countries, with the vast majority of Venezuelans residing in the northern cities and the capital.

Tourism has grown significantly in recent decades, owing to the country's favorable geographical location, the diversity of landscapes, the richness of plant and wildlife, artistic expressions, and the country's privileged tropical climate, which allows each region to enjoy pleasant weather throughout the year.

Margarita Island

Margarita Island is one of the most popular vacation spots for fun and relaxation. It's an island with stunning beaches perfect for extreme sports and castles, fortifications, and churches of considerable cultural significance.

Los Roques Archipelago

The Los Roques Archipelago is a set of islands and keys that make up one of the country's most popular tourist destinations. Morrocoy is a national park formed by small keys close to the mainland that has quickly emerged as one of the most popular tourist destinations in the Venezuelan Caribbean due to its exquisite crystalline beaches.

Canaima National Park

Canaima National Park covers 12 sq. miles (30,000 km^2) and is the world's sixth largest national park due to its vastness. It's located on the border of Guyana and Brazil. Tepuis, or rock plateaus, cover around 65 percent of the park. This is a one-of-a-kind ecological ecosystem that also has a lot of geological importance. Its dramatic scenery is dominated by steep cliffs and waterfalls, including Angel Falls, the world's highest waterfall at 3,212 ft. (1,002 meters).

Breakfast

Venezuelan Sticky Buns (Golfeados)

Preparation time: 15 minutes
Cook time: 27 minutes
Nutrition facts (per serving): 314 Cal (6g fat, 20g protein, 2g fiber)

These sticky buns are loved by all, young and adult. They're simple and quick to make. They're great to serve at dinner tables with stews, pulled meats, and soups.

Ingredients (6 servings)

Dough

¾ cup warm milk
2 (¼ oz.) active dry yeast
¼ cup sugar
2 tablespoon dark brown sugar
3 cups all-purpose flour
1 teaspoon salt
2 large eggs, beaten
1 tablespoon honey
1 teaspoon pure vanilla extract
4 tablespoon unsalted butter, softened
1 tablespoon aniseed
Vegetable oil for greasing bowl

Filling

8 oz. firm white cheese, grated
½ cup packed dark brown sugar
1 teaspoon ground cinnamon
1 teaspoon aniseed
4 tablespoon unsalted butter, softened

Glaze (Mel ado)

1 ½ cups brown sugar

1 cup water

Preparation

Mix the yeast with ¼ cup warm milk and ¼ teaspoon sugar in a small bowl and leave for 10 minutes. Add the flour with rest of the dough ingredients to a stand mixing bowl. Stir in the yeast mixture and then mix well until it makes smooth dough. Cover and leave the dough for 1 hour. Mix 2 tablespoon of cheese with aniseed, cinnamon, and brown sugar in a bowl. Cover and refrigerate the filling for 30 minutes.

Roll out the dough on a floured surface into 16x14 inch rectangle. Brush this dough with butter and add the cheese mixture at the center leaving ½ inch borders. Roll the dough to make a 16-inch-long log. Cut the log into 12 rolls and place them in a baking sheet lined with parchment paper.

Bake the rolls for 20 minutes in the oven at 350 degrees F. Prepare the glaze, mix brown sugar and rest of the glaze ingredients in a saucepan then cook for 7 minutes. Allow the glaze to cool and pour over the baked rolls. Sprinkle cheese on top. Serve.

Arepitas Dulce's (Sweet Arepas)

Preparation time: 15 minutes
Cook time: 10 minutes
Nutrition facts (per serving): 347 Cal (5g fat, 7g protein, 5g fiber)

A dessert that has no parallel, the Venezuelan sweet arepas are made with panela, corn flour and flour to create a heavenly combination.

Ingredients (6 servings)
Panela Mix
1 cup panela
¼ cup water

Arepas
1 cup pre-cooked corn flour for arepas
¼ cup all-purpose flour
1 pinch salt
½ cup panela mix
½ cup water
4 cups vegetable oil for frying

Instructions
In a small cooking pot, mix the panela with water over medium heat, until it becomes sticky like honey. Set it aside and allow it to cool. In a bowl, mix the flour and the pinch of salt. Make a hole in the middle, and add the panela mix and water. Mix well with a fork. Knead for five minutes. The dough should be a tiny bit drier than cookie dough. If too dry, add a little bit of water. Make small balls from the dough and flatten each ball slightly

with both hands, making them into mini-arepas. You could also flatten them by placing between a plastic wrapper using a plate. Arepas should be ⅙ to ⅛ of an inch thick. In a deep-frying pan, heat vegetable oil over medium heat.

Place the mini arepas in the hot oil, showering them in the oil. Make sure they're evenly golden. Once ready, drain in a paper towel. Eat immediately with grated queso blanco or your choice of topping.

Green Plantain Pancake

Preparation time: 15 minutes
Cook time: 10 minutes
Nutrition facts (per serving): 221 Cal (3 g fat, 4 g protein, 2.8g fiber)

Yes, you can make something as delicious as these Venezuelan plantain pancakes by using only basic ingredients and some simple techniques.

Ingredients (6 servings)
2 medium green plantain, peeled
10 oz. of fresh white cheese, cubed
Oil, for frying
Salt, to taste

Sauce
2 plum tomatoes, chopped
3 scallions, sliced
¼ cup cilantro, chopped
Salt, to taste
1 pinch of cayenne pepper
2 tablespoon butter

Preparation
Begin by making the sauce. In a small sauce pan, add all the ingredients, except the cayenne pepper. Stir to combine, cover with lid, and cook on low heat while working on the pancakes. Fill a medium-sized pot to cook the plantains. Fill just enough water to cover the plantains. Bring to a boil and cook the plantains until fork tender. Then transfer it all in a large bowl

and mash until smooth. Use your hands to get a smoother texture. Place a piece of plastic wrap on your work surface. Grab a piece of the mashed plantain and roll it into a ball. Then pat it down to a pancake form. Place a piece of cheese in the middle. Grab another plantain ball and place it on top.

With the help of the plastic wrap, combine both pieces of plantains to make one pancake by patting it down or with a rolling-pin. Then set aside. Repeat this procedure until all mashed plantain is used up. Fry the pancakes on medium heat 2-3 minutes on each side. Have ready a plate double lined with paper towel to absorb any excess oil.

Revert back to the sauce. It should be saucy by this point. Add in the cayenne pepper before serving. Serve the pancakes warm.

Egg-Stuffed Arepas (Arepas De Huevo)

Preparation time: 10 minutes
Cook time: 15 minutes
Nutrition facts (per serving): 141 Cal (10g fat, 2g protein, 1.1g fiber)

Arepa is a Venezuelan version of pita pockets. You can serve them as flatbread or stuff them with egg filling to enjoy at breakfast.

Ingredients (6 servings)
1 cup hot water
½ teaspoon food coloring
1 teaspoon salt
½ teaspoon sugar
1 cup white pre-cooked cornmeal
6 large eggs
Oil, for frying
Black pepper and salt to taste

Preparation
In a suitable mixing bowl, combine the boiling water, food coloring, salt, and sugar. Stir everything together thoroughly. Stir in the cornmeal with a wooden spoon or spatula while slowly adding. When the cornmeal has absorbed all of the water, knead the dough with your hands until it is smooth and lump-free. Make 6 equal balls out of the dough. Place one ball in a tortilla press lined with plastic and flatten it to a thickness of approximately 14 inches. Make sure the arepa is evenly flattened. Place the arepa gently in 350°F hot oil and allow it to drop to the bottom. Once the

arepa has risen to the surface, use a large spoon to cover it with additional oil for about 2-3 minutes. The arepa will puff up as a result of this.

After that, remove it from the oil and drain it on paper towels. Continue the process for each arepa. Season with black pepper and salt to taste and crack one egg into a cup with a sharp lip. Once the arepa is cold enough to handle, create a small pocket on the side of the arepa with a sharp knife about 112 inches broad. After that, carefully pour the seasoned egg inside and return the arepa to the heated oil. Cook for 2-3 minutes, or until the egg is fully cooked. Repeat with each additional arepa. Drain the arepa on paper towels after removing it from the oil. Serve right away.

Venezuelan Sweet Plantains

Preparation time: 10 minutes
Cook time: 10 minutes
Nutrition facts (per serving): 202 Cal (7g fat, 6g protein, 1.3g fiber)

If you love to have a different variety of crispy plantains in your menu, then these sweet plantains are perfect pairings with all the breakfast eggs, frittatas, or bacon.

Ingredients (4 servings)
4 ripe plantains, peeled and sliced
2 tablespoons butter
2 tablespoons oil
2 tablespoons sugar
¼ teaspoon ground cinnamon

Preparation
Set a suitable skillet with butter and oil over medium-high heat. Sear the plantains for 2 minutes per side. Reduce its heat and drizzle cinnamon and sugar over the plantains. Cover them with a lid and cook for 10 minutes. Flip the plantains once after cooked halfway through. Serve.

Venezuelan Milk Truffles (Papitas De Leche)

Preparation time: 10 minutes
Nutrition facts (per serving): 199 Cal (5g fat, 7g protein, 0g fiber)

The Venezuelan milk truffles are great to serve with all types of egg dishes and bacon. They have an appealing milky taste that goes with everything.

Ingredients (6 servings)
2 cups powdered milk
1 (14 oz.) can sweetened condensed milk
1 cup confectioner's sugar
36 cloves

Preparation
Mix the milk with the sugar in a bowl. Stir in the condensed milk and mix well until it makes smooth dough. Divide the dough into 36 pieces. Roll each piece into a ball and place them onto a baking sheet. Insert a clove in each ball. Serve.

Venezuelan Scrambled Eggs (Perico Venezolano)

Preparation time: 15 minutes
Cook time: 6 minutes
Nutrition facts (per serving): 312 Cal (16g fat, 18g protein, 7g fiber)

The Venezuelan scrambled eggs are famous for their delicious flavor and loaded texture made from egg, onion, bell pepper, garlic, and tomatoes.

Ingredients (4 servings)
2 tablespoons oil
1 onion, chopped
1 bell pepper, chopped
2 garlic cloves, minced
2 tomatoes, seeded and chopped
6 eggs, beaten
Black pepper and salt, to taste

Preparation
Sauté the onion, garlic, and bell pepper with oil in a skillet over medium high heat for 4 minutes. Stir in the tomatoes and cook for 4 minutes. Reduce its heat and stir in the black pepper, salt, and eggs and cook for 2-3 minutes while scrambling it. Serve.

Venezuelan Cocada

Preparation time: 10 minutes
Cook time: 7 minutes
Nutrition facts (per serving): 378 Cal (16g fat, 4g protein, 2g fiber)

This Venezuelan cocada tastes heavenly when prepared at home. Serve it fresh with your favorite egg meal on the side.

Ingredients (2 servings)

2 cups fresh coconut meat
1 ½ cup whole milk
½ cup sweetened condensed milk
1 teaspoon pure vanilla extract
2 cups ice

Preparation

Blend the coconut meat with vanilla, milk, and condensed milk in a blender for 3 minutes. Strain this mixture through a fine sieve. Blend this mixture with ice in the blender for 2 minutes. Garnish with cinnamon and serve.

Casabe (Cassava Bread)

Preparation time: 15 minutes
Cook time: 10 minutes
Nutrition facts (per serving): 410 Cal (6g fat, 20g protein, 1.4g fiber)

Try this cassava bread for your breakfast, and you'll forget about the rest. The recipe is simple and gives you lots of nutrients in one place.

Ingredients (6 servings)
1 lb. cassava, peeled and grated
Parmesan casaba, to taste
⅓ cup of Parmesan, grated
½ teaspoon of salt
2 garlic cloves crushed into a paste
¼ cup of olive oil

Preparation
Spread the cassava shreds on a baking sheet and refrigerate for 4 hours. Stir them every hour. Place a pan over medium heat. Sauté the cassava with oil in the pan for 1 minute. Mix the Parmesan with cassava, salt, and garlic in a bowl. Spread this mixture in a greased pan and bake until golden brown. Serve.

Potato Hash with Linguica

Preparation time: 15 minutes
Cook time: 12 minutes
Nutrition facts (per serving): 256 Cal (16g fat, 9g protein, 6g fiber)

This potato hash is another nutritious yet simple meal for the breakfast table. It delivers lots of nutrients and fibers to the table, along with healthy ingredients that are cooked together in a tempting combination.

Ingredients (4 servings)

½-lb. linguiça sausage, diced
2 lbs. russet potatoes, diced
Cooking oil, for frying
1 yellow onion, diced
2 garlic cloves, minced
¾ cup canned garbanzo beans, drained
2 teaspoons sweet paprika
¾ teaspoon smoked paprika
1 ½ teaspoon salt
¼ teaspoon black pepper
¾ cup roasted red peppers, diced
⅓ cup green olives, halved
⅓ cup black olives, halved
4 large eggs
¼ cup parsley, chopped

Preparation

Sauté the linguica in a skillet until brown and then transfer to a plate while leaving the drippings in the skillet. Stir in the potatoes and sauté until golden brown. Transfer the potatoes to a plate. Add the oil and the onions to the same skillet, then sauté until brown. Stir in the garlic and sauté for almost 30 seconds. Stir in the garbanzo beans and sauté for almost 1 minute. Return the linguica and potatoes to the skillet and then stir in the rest of the ingredients. Make four wells in this prepared mixture and crack one egg into each well. Transfer this skillet to the oven and bake for 10 minutes at 400 degrees F. Garnish with parsley. Serve.

Venezuelan Corn Pancakes (Cachapas)

Preparation time: 15 minutes
Cook time: 12 minutes
Nutrition facts (per serving): 87 Cal (5g fat, 1g protein, 5g fiber)

If you haven't tried the corn pancakes recipe before, then here comes a simple and easy to cook recipe that you can recreate at home in no time with minimum efforts.

Ingredients (4 servings)

2 cups corn
1 egg
½ cup milk
4 tablespoons masa harina
1 tablespoon sugar
1 teaspoon salt
2 tablespoons butter
8 oz. fresh mozzarella, sliced

Preparation

Blend the sugar, salt, corn flour, milk, egg, and corn in a blender. Leave this mixture for 10 minutes. Set a 5 ½ inch frying pan over medium heat and grease it with butter. Pour about ⅓ cup of this batter in the pan and spread it evenly. Cook the pancake for 2-3 minutes per side. Cook more pancakes in the same way. Place a mozzarella slice on top of each pancake and fold in half. Serve.

Appetizers

Beef And Potato Empanadas Vallunas

Preparation time: 15 minutes
Cook time: 1 hour 40 minutes
Nutrition facts (per serving): 201 Cal (6g fat, 4g protein, 0.6g fiber)

The Venezuelan empanadas have no parallel. They're quick and simple to make at home if you have beef chuck and other filling ingredients at home.

Ingredients (6 servings)
Filling
1 beef chuck
3 green onions chopped
¼ white onion
2 whole garlic cloves
1 beef bouillon
Salt and black pepper, to taste
Water
1 lb. papas criollas

Tomato Sauce (Guiso)
3 tablespoon olive oil
3 green onions chopped
2 garlic cloves minced
2 medium seedless tomatoes chopped
1 teaspoon ground cumin
1 teaspoon food coloring
Salt and black pepper, to taste
1 cup water

Dough

4½ cups hot water

1½ teaspoon food coloring

2 tablespoon vegetable oil

Salt to, taste

4 cups pre-cooked cornmeal (to make arepas)

Additional vegetable oil, for frying

Preparation

Add the beef and the rest of the filling ingredients to a pressure cooker. Cover and seal the lid, cook for 1 ½ hours, and then release the pressure completely. Remove the lid and shred the beef. Cook this mixture until it makes a dry filling. Mix all the dough ingredients in a bowl. Make 2 tablespoon sized balls from this dough. Spread each dough ball into a flat round and add a tablespoon of filling at the center and fold in half. Press the edges with a fork and deep fry the empanadas until golden brown. Serve warm.

Venezuelan Black Beans

Preparation time: 15 minutes
Cook time: 12 minutes
Nutrition facts (per serving): 230 Cal (22g fat, 10g protein, 1.4g fiber)

If you haven't tried the Venezuelan black beans before, then here comes a simple and easy to cook recipe that you can easily prepare and cook at home in no time with minimum efforts.

Ingredients (6 servings)

1 (16-oz.) bag of dried black beans
1 green bell pepper, chopped
3 tablespoon vegetable oil
1 large onion, chopped
4 garlic cloves, minced
2 tablespoon molasses
1 tablespoon cumin
½ teaspoon Worcestershire sauce
4 slices bacon
2 cups chicken stock
1 teaspoon salt
½ teaspoon black pepper

Preparation

Soak the beans overnight and rinse. Add the chopped bell peppers, beans, and enough water to cover them to a pan. Cook on a simmer until the beans are cooked and soft. Sauté the bacon in a skillet until crispy. Stir in the chopped onion and garlic then sauté until soft. Stir in the brown sugar and cumin and cook for 1 minute. Blend the beans with the onion mixture in a blender until chunky. Stir in the black pepper, salt, and Worcestershire sauce and then mix well. Serve.

Chicken Turnovers (Pasteles De Pollo)

Preparation time: 15 minutes
Cook time: 45 minutes
Nutrition facts (per serving): 118 Cal (17g fat, 1g protein, 8g fiber)

Chicken turnovers are the main specialty of the Venezuelan snack menu. Now you can try them with tomato sauce.

Ingredients (6 servings)

Chicken

2-3 green onions, chopped
¼ white onion
2 garlic cloves
1 medium half chicken breast
2 large russet potatoes, peeled and cubed
Salt, to taste

Guiso

3 tablespoon olive oil
3 green onions chopped, stalks only
2 garlic cloves chopped
2 medium tomatoes chopped
1 teaspoon ground cumin
1 teaspoon food coloring
Salt, to taste
1 cup water

Dough

4½ cups hot water

1 chicken bouillon

2 teaspoon food coloring

2 tablespoon vegetable oil

Salt, to taste

4 cups pre-cooked cornmeal

Vegetable oil, for frying

Preparation

In a suitable saucepan, combine the chicken breast, green onions, white onion, and garlic. Add enough water to cover the chicken. Cover and bring the pot to a boil over high heat. Reduce the heat to medium low and then simmer for 30-35 minutes, or until the chicken cooked. Remove the chicken from the pot and set it aside to cool. Set it aside after shredding it.

In a suitable saucepan, cover the potatoes with water and season with salt. Bring the pot to a boil over high heat, covered. Reduce the heat to medium low once it boils and cook for 20-25 minutes, or until the potatoes are cooked.

Drain the cooked potatoes and mash them with a fork or a potato masher before setting them aside. Pour the boiling water into a suitable mixing bowl to produce the dough. Combine the chicken bouillon, food coloring, vegetable oil, and salt in a suitable mixing bowl. Gradually stir in by adding the pre-cooked cornmeal. Knead until it's soft and silky with your hands. Allow for 10 minutes of resting time after covering with plastic wrap or a clean kitchen towel.

In a suitable skillet, heat the olive oil over medium heat. Cook for 2 minutes after adding the green onion and garlic. Cook, stirring occasionally, for 7-8 minutes, or until the tomatoes are softened. Cumin and food coloring are added as seasonings. Season with black pepper and salt to taste after adding 1 cup of water. Now add the shredded chicken and the mashed potatoes and stir well to cover them with the tomato sauce. Taste for seasoning and add more salt.

Preheat the oil to 350 degrees F. To assemble the turnovers, make small balls of masa of about 1 inch in diameter. Cover a tortilla press with plastic wrap, insert a small ball in the center, and press to produce a disc; set aside. Repeat with the other little ball. Fill one of the discs with roughly 1-2 tablespoons of filling, leaving a 12 inch border. On top of the filling, place the second disc. To seal the edges, press them together with your fingers, then crimp the edge with your thumb. Continue in this manner until all of the turnovers have been assembled. Deep fry the turnovers for around 7-8 minutes or until golden brown in the preheated oil. To ensure that they cook evenly on both sides, rotate them halfway through the cooking procedure. They should be drained on paper towels and served right away.

Venezuelan Arepas

Preparation time: 10 minutes
Cook time: 15 minutes
Nutrition facts (per serving): 425 Cal (28g fat, 33g protein, 2g fiber)

Have you tried the Venezuelan arepas before? Well, now you can enjoy this unique and flavorsome combination by cooking this recipe at home.

Ingredients (6 servings)

2 cups warm water
1 tablespoon oil
1 teaspoon salt
2 cups masa arepa

Preparation

Mix salt, water, and oil in a large bowl. Stir in the masa arepa and then mix well. Cover this bowl and leave for 10 minutes. Divide this dough into 6 equal pieces and shape each into a ½ inch disc. Set a cast iron griddle over medium high heat and grease it with oil. Sear the arepas for 5 minutes per side. Cook all the arepas in the same way. Serve.

Venezuelan Guasacaca

Preparation time: 10 minutes
Nutrition facts (per serving): 217 Cal (14g fat, 9g protein, 0.3g fiber)

Guasacaca is an avocado dip which tastes much like a guacamole but with a twist of Worcestershire sauce. Keep it ready in the refrigerator to serve.

Ingredients (6 servings)

3 ripe avocados, peeled and seeded
1 medium onion, chopped
½ green pepper, seeded and chopped
1 garlic clove, peeled
½ cup fresh cilantro leave
⅓ cup white vinegar
1 tablespoon salt or to taste
¼ teaspoon black pepper
1 teaspoon Worcestershire sauce
1 cup corn oil

Preparation

Mash the avocados in a salad bowl, stir in rest of the ingredients, and then mix evenly. Serve.

Venezuelan Cuajada Cheese

Preparation time: 10 minutes
Cook time: 10 minutes
Nutrition facts (per serving): 396 Cal (13g fat, 22g protein, 4g fiber)

This cuajada cheese is served as a bread spread or as a side meal. Enjoy this cheese with sliced berries and compote on top.

Ingredients (8 servings)
1 gallon pasteurized milk
¼ teaspoon calcium chloride
1 packet Mesophilic Starter Culture
⅛ teaspoon vegetable rennet

Preparation
Add the milk to a suitable bowl and heat it to 97 degrees F. Add the calcium chloride and starter culture to the milk. Mix for 2 minutes and then leave for 45 minutes. Mix the rennet with ¼ cup water and add to the milk. Leave for 45 minutes. Cut the curd into cubes and strain using a cheesecloth. Transfer to a mold and press the curd. Refrigerate for 15 minutes and serve.

Fried Plantain Strips

Preparation time: 5 minutes
Cook time: 10 minutes
Nutrition facts (per serving): 413 Cal (18g fat, 10g protein, 6g fiber)

Venezuelan plantain strips are one of the most delicious snacks to sample. You can try different variations for its toppings as well.

Ingredients (8 servings)
4 ripe plantains
¼ cup vegetable oil
Salt, to taste

Preparation
Cut the pointy tips off the ends of the plantains using a sharp knife. Be sure that each plantain's pointed ends are trimmed off. In numerous places along the length of the plantain, add a score that cuts through the peel. Each piece should be cut in half lengthwise twice more, yielding four long slices from each plantain.

In a heavy skillet over medium heat, heat the oil and cook the plantain slices until dark golden brown on both sides. Sprinkle salt on the slices after draining them on a paper towel. Warm it up and enjoy it!

Yuca Fries

Preparation time: 10 minutes
Cook time: 10 minutes
Nutrition facts (per serving): 179 Cal (16g fat, 15g protein, 3g fiber)

The Venezuelan yuca fries platter is an interesting snack to serve at the snack table, and it tastes divine. Use this quick and simple recipe to get it ready in no time.

Ingredients (6 servings)
3 lbs. fresh yuca (cassava), peeled and cut into sticks
Salt, to taste
3 cups vegetable oil
Avocado Sauce (Guasacaca), to serve
Cilantro Mojo, to serve

Preparation
Heat 3 cups cooking oil in a deep pan over medium heat. Deep fry the yuca fries in the oil until golden brown. Remove the prepared fries from the oil using a slotted spoon. Serve with avocado sauce and cilantro mojo.

Spinach And Cheese Hand Pies

Preparation time: 15 minutes
Cook time: 20 minutes
Nutrition facts (per serving): 381 Cal (5g fat, 3g protein, 6g fiber)

If you haven't tried spinach and cheese hand pies before, then here comes a simple and easy to cook recipe that you can serve at home easily.

Ingredients (6 servings)
1 tablespoon olive oil
½ medium onion, chopped
1 garlic clove, chopped
¾ cup ricotta cheese
½ cup shredded mozzarella cheese
¼ cup cream cheese
¼ cup grated Parmesan cheese
½ teaspoon Italian herbs
1 teaspoon salt
¼ teaspoon black pepper
5 oz. frozen spinach, thawed and squeezed
2 sheets of puff pastry, thawed
¼ cup milk

Preparation
Sauté the onion with the oil in a saucepan for 3 minutes, add garlic, and sauté for 1 minute. Mix the ricotta, black pepper, herbs, Parmesan cheese, cream cheese, and mozzarella cheese in a large bowl. Stir in spinach and onion mixture. Mix evenly. At 350 degrees F, preheat your oven. Layer a

cookie sheet with parchment paper. Roll out the thawed puff pastry and cut 10 (3 ½ inch) circles out of it. Brush 5 rounds with milk and add a spoonful of spinach filling at the center. Place the remaining rounds on to crimp the edges with a fork. Place these puffs in a baking sheet and brush them with milk. Bake for 20 minutes in the oven until golden brown. Serve warm.

Bacon Choripan With Chimichurri Sauce

Preparation time: 15 minutes
Cook time: 10 minutes
Nutrition facts (per serving): 252 Cal (13g fat, 24g protein, 4g fiber)

The Venezuelan bacon choripan is a delight to serve at the breakfast table. It's known for its comforting effects, and the meal offers a very energizing combination of ingredients.

Ingredients (6 servings)
Chimichurri Sauce
½ cup parsley leaves
¼ cup cilantro leaves
1 shallot, peeled and chopped
1 small red sweet pepper, deveined and seeds removed
3 garlic cloves, peeled
1-2 teaspoon chili pepper flakes
2 tablespoon red wine vinegar
1 tablespoon fresh lemon juice
½ cup light olive oil
Black pepper and salt to taste

Choripan
8 slices hickory smoked bacon
4 chorizos, fully cooked
4 crusty hot dog buns
8 slices cheddar cheese
4 fried eggs

Preparation

Blend all the chimichurri sauce ingredients in a blender. At 400 degrees F, preheat your oven. Sauté the bacon in a suitable skillet until brown and crispy and then transfer to a plate lined with paper towel. Sauté the chorizo in a skillet until brown and then transfer to a plate. Cut the bread in half lengthwise. Top half of the bread slices with 2 cheese slices and then transfer the bread to a baking sheet. Bake for 3 minutes until the cheese is melted. Add 2 slices of bacon and 1 chorizo on top of each bread slice. Pour a dollop of chimichurri sauce on top. Add one fried egg on top and set the remaining bread slice on top. Serve warm.

Venezuelan Sweet Corn Fritters (Mandocas)

Preparation time: 10 minutes
Cook time: 5 minutes
Nutrition facts (per serving): 260 Cal (3g fat, 3g protein, 11g fiber)

Try this Venezuelan sweet corn fritters with your favorite sauces on the side. You can add corn to the fritter batter to enjoy a chunky texture.

Ingredients (4 servings)

Syrup

2 ¼ cup water
1 ¼ cup papelon, grated
2 allspice berries
1 cinnamon stick
2 teaspoon anise seeds

Dough

2 cups Harina pan
2 cups papelon syrup
1 cup queso blanco (white hard cheese) grated
Corn oil, for deep-frying

Preparation

Boil all the syrup ingredients in a saucepan and cook for 30 minutes on a simmer with occasional stirring. Discard the berries, cinnamon, and anise seeds. Allow the syrup to cool down. Mix harina, the prepared syrup, and queso blanco in a bowl to make the dough. Divide this dough into 20 equal sized balls. Spread each piece into a 6 inches long cylinder and bring the two ends together to make a tear loop. Repeat this same step with the remaining dough. Deep fry the dough in hot oil at 375 degrees F, for 5 minutes. Transfer the fritters to a plate lined with a paper towel. Serve.

Venezuelan Sweet Corn Sauce

Preparation time: 15 minutes
Nutrition facts (per serving): 289 Cal (13g fat, 3g protein, 2g fiber)

It's about time to try the sweet corn sauce with all your favorite snacks and delights. Now you can prepare quickly using corn kernels.

Ingredients (8 servings)

1 oz. can sweet corn kernels
3 tablespoon cream cheese
5 tablespoon mayonnaise
2 tablespoon honey
2 tablespoon corn oil
1 tablespoon mustard
½ teaspoon salt
1 pinch black pepper

Preparation

Blend the corn kernels with cream cheese, mayonnaise, honey, corn oil, mustard, black pepper, and salt in a blender. Pass this sauce through a mesh strainer. Serve.

Loaded Reina Pepiada Wraps

Preparation time: 10 minutes
Cook time: 10 minutes
Nutrition facts (per serving): 162 Cal (13g fat, 15g protein, 2g fiber)

If you can't think of anything to cook and make in a short time, then these avocado and chicken filled flatbreads are the perfect choice because of their great taste and texture.

Ingredients (6 servings)
1 ripe avocado, peeled and chopped
¼ cup onion, chopped
1 cup mayonnaise
Black pepper, to taste
3 cups cooked chicken, shredded
4 flat-out flatbreads
4 leaves of lettuce
1 tomato, sliced

Preparation
Blend the avocado with black pepper, mayonnaise, and onion in a food processor. Mix this mayo mixture with shredded chicken in a bowl. Spread each flatbread on the working surface top each with chicken mixture, tomato slices, and lettuce leaves and then wrap the flatbread. Serve.

Venezuelan Cheese and Ham Empanadas

Preparation time: 15 minutes
Cook time: 10 minutes
Nutrition facts (per serving): 357 Cal (32g fat, 15g protein, 1.4g fiber)

Impress with these Venezuelan cheese and ham empanadas on the menu. The combination of cheese and ham filled inside the empanadas is bliss for all cheese lovers like me!

Ingredients (6 servings)

Filling

1 ½ cup Mozzarella Cheese, shredded
1 cup sliced ham, chopped

Dough

2 cups water
1 teaspoon salt
1 tablespoon sugar
1 ½ cups harina, pre-cooked white maize meal
¼ cup all-purpose flour
1 teaspoon baking powder
Oil, to fry
Guasacasa, for serving

Preparation

Mix the shredded cheese and ham in a medium bowl. Mix the flour with rest of the dough ingredients in a bowl until it makes a smooth dough. Divide the dough into 12 equal portions and roll each ball into a 5 inched circle. Add a tablespoon of the filling at the center of each circle and fold in half. Press the edges of the dough to seal the filling inside. Set a suitable skillet with 2 inches of vegetable oil over medium heat. Deep fry the empanadas until golden brown for 2 minutes per side. Remove the empanadas to a plate lined with paper towel. Serve warm.

Venezuelan Cachitos De Jamon

Preparation time: 15 minutes
Cook time: 25 minutes
Nutrition facts (per serving): 206 Cal (29g fat, 4g protein, 0.1g fiber)

The appetizing cachitos de jamon make great addition to the menu, and they look enticing when served at the table. You can serve this crispy delight with tomato sauce.

Ingredients (8 servings)

¼ oz. active dry yeast
1 cup warm water
2 tablespoon granulated sugar
2 tablespoon light-brown sugar
1 tablespoon vegetable oil
1 teaspoon salt
1 ½ cups bread flour
1 ¼ cups all-purpose flour
1 lb. lean ham, chopped
4 tablespoons of butter, melted

Preparation

Mix 1 cup warm water with ½ tablespoon sugar, and yeast in a mixer and then leave for 10 minutes. Transfer this mixture to a stand mixer. Add remaining sugar, salt, oil, brown sugar and bread flour then mix on low speed for 8 minutes until evenly incorporated. Transfer this dough to a greased bowl, cover with a plastic wrap and leave for 2 hours. Punch down the dough and divide it into 2 equal parts. Spread each portion into a 16 inch round. Cut 6 equal triangles from this sheet. Add 4 tablespoon of ham at the center of each triangle. Fold the corners and pinch them to seal. Roll the triangle into a crescent. Place all the crescents on a baking sheet and bake for 25 minutes at 375 degrees F. Brush with melted butter and serve.

Yuca Frita

Preparation time: 5 minutes
Cook time: 15 minutes
Nutrition facts (per serving): 204 Cal (9g fat, 6g protein, 1.7g fiber)

These hearty yuca fritas at the snack table can be enjoyed with a delicious avocado sauce or some other condiment.

Ingredients (6 servings)
2 lbs. yuca (cassava) root
Water, for boiling
Oil, for deep frying
Salt, to taste

Preparation
A big saucepan of salted water should be brought to a boil. Peel the yuca's rough brown skin and chop it into large parts. The stringy middle should be avoided. Cook for 15 to 20 minutes after adding the yuca to the boiling water. Drain the yuca and spread it out on a clean towel. While the oil is heating up, let the steam dry for 10 to 15 minutes. Heat the oil for deep frying until it shimmers, or until a deep frying thermometer reads 365 degrees F. Fry the yuca in batches until a golden brown color is achieved. Place on a paper towel-lined platter and keep warm in the oven while you finish the rest of the batches. Serve with a pinch of salt.

Venezuelan Nata

Preparation time: 15 minutes
Cook time: 15 minutes
Nutrition facts (per serving): 279 Cal (5.2g fat, 2.8g protein, 3g fiber)

If you haven't tried the Venezuelan creamy spread, then you must now as it offers no parallel in taste and texture.

Ingredients (6 servings)
2 cups heavy cream
1 tablespoon lemon juice
½ teaspoon salt

Preparation
Blend cream in a stand mixer for 5 minutes. Stir in the salt and the lemon juice and then beat for 7 minutes until it makes a soft peak. Serve.

Traditional Avocado Sauce

Preparation time: 15 minutes
Nutrition facts (per serving): 232 Cal (11g fat, 23g protein, 3g fiber)

Are you looking for a refreshing sauce to serve with snacks and meals? Then this avocado sauce is the perfect fit for you.

Ingredients (8 servings)
2 big ripe avocados, peeled and seeded
1 small onion, chopped
½ green pepper, seeded and chopped
2 garlic cloves, peeled
6 tablespoon fresh lime juice
¾ cup avocado oil
2 teaspoon salt
¼ teaspoon black pepper
½ cup fresh cilantro leave

Preparation
Blend the avocados with salt and rest of the ingredients in a blender. Serve.

Venezuelan Pan De Jamon

Preparation time: 15 minutes
Cook time: 45 minutes
Nutrition facts (per serving): 246 Cal (23g fat, 12g protein, 3g fiber)

This baked dough stuffed with green olives, ham, and raisins is another Venezuelan-inspired delight that you should definitely prepare on this cuisine. Serve with flavorsome dips or sauces.

Ingredients (6 servings)

Dough

⅓ cup milk
⅓ cup water
2 cups 1 tablespoon bread flour
1 tablespoon granulated sugar
1 tablespoon instant yeast
½ teaspoon salt
1 egg
2 tablespoon unsalted butter, melted
1 whole egg
1 tablespoon water
Melted butter for brushing

Filling

2 cups pimiento-stuffed green olives, drained and sliced
1 lb. ham
1 ½ cups raisins
¼ cup papelon syrup

Preparation

Layer a baking tray with a parchment paper sheet then grease it with cooking oil. Mix milk and water in a bowl and heat for 30 seconds. Add salt, yeast, sugar, and flour to a stand mixer. Stir in the melted butter, egg, and milk mixture and then mix for 10 minutes on medium-high heat until it makes a sticky dough. Knead this dough on a floured surface then transfer it to a greased bowl. Cover and leave it for 2 hours. Punch down the dough and roll it into 15x13 inch rectangle. Set a row of whole olives on the upper edge of the rectangle and slice the rest of the olives. Place the ham slices over the dough while overlapping each other. Add the sliced olives and raisins on top. Add the papelon syrup on. Roll the dough while keeping the filling inside. Place the roll in the baking sheet with its seam side down. Cover it with a damp towel and leave for 1 hour. At 350 degrees F, preheat your oven. Brush the roll with egg wash and bake for 45 minutes. Brush with melted butter and slice. Serve.

Tostones

Preparation time: 15 minutes
Cook time: 10 minutes
Nutrition facts (per serving): 146 Cal (21g fat, 9g protein, 4.1g fiber)

These tostones are everyone's favorite go-to meal when it comes to serving Venezuelan meals. In turn, you can prepare them in no time.

Ingredients (6 servings)
2 large green plantains, peeled and sliced
2 cups vegetable oil for frying
¼ teaspoon salt

Preparation
Add vegetable oil to a deep-frying pan and heat it to 325 degrees F. Slice the plantains and smash them. Deep fry the plantains until golden brown. Transfer the plantains to a plate lined with a paper towel. Drizzle salt over the tostones and serve.

Venezuelan Tequeños

Preparation time: 10 minutes
Cook time: 10 minutes
Nutrition facts (per serving): 102 Cal (5g fat, 5g protein, 2g fiber)

The Venezuelan tequenos offer another most popular snack in Venezuelan Cuisine, and they exude great taste from the cheese stick filling.

Ingredients (12 servings)
2 cups all-purpose flour
½ teaspoon salt
¼ teaspoon baking power
¼ cup water
¼ cup vegetable oil
¼ cup milk
1 tablespoon brown sugar
1 block semi-hard white cheese for frying
Vegetable oil, for frying

Spicy Pink Sauce
1 cup mayonnaise
⅓ cup ketchup
1 tablespoon lemon juice
1 teaspoon Worcestershire sauce
1 tablespoon brandy
½ teaspoon cayenne pepper

Preparation

Blend the mayonnaise, ketchup, lemon juice, Worcestershire sauce, brandy, and cayenne pepper in a bowl. Mix the flour with baking powder and salt in a bowl of stand mixer. Stir in the brown sugar, milk, vegetable oil, and water and mix for 7 minutes on medium speed. Wrap the dough with a plastic sheet and refrigerate for 30 minutes. Knead the dough for 3 minutes. Roll out the dough into 12x15 inch rectangle and cut 12 (1 inch) wide strips. Slice the cheese block into 6 equal portions and cut each in half to get 12 cheese sticks. Wrap each stick with a dough strip. Deep fry the covered cheese in hot oil at 350 degrees F until golden brown. Transfer the tequenos to a plate lined with paper towel. Serve them with the pink sauce.

Salads

Venezuelan Kale Salad

Preparation time: 10 minutes
Nutrition facts (per serving): 276 Cal (17g fat, 7g protein, 3g fiber)

It's almost if the Venezuelan menu is incomplete without this kale salad. Made with kale, cabbage, and carrots, it adds lots of nutritional value to your life here.

Ingredients (4 servings)
2 x 7 ½ oz. packs curly kale, sliced
¼ small red cabbage, shredded
2 carrots, peeled and julienned
1 avocado, sliced
7 ½ oz. cherry tomatoes, halved
4 tablespoons of extra-virgin olive oil
½ orange, juiced
2 tablespoons of red wine vinegar

Preparation
Toss the kales with the rest of the ingredients in a salad bowl. Serve.

Venezuelan Potato Chicken Salad (Ensalada De Galina)

Preparation time: 15 minutes
Cook time: 35 minutes
Nutrition facts (per serving): 160 Cal (15g fat, 1g protein, 2g fiber)

The Venezuelan potato chicken salad is famous for its crispy texture, unique taste, and delectable aroma, and now you can bring those exotic flavors home with this recipe.

Ingredients (6 servings)

2 chicken breasts
3 big potatoes, peeled and diced
3 big carrots, peeled and diced
¼ cup green peas
1 green apple, peeled and diced
5 tablespoons mayonnaise
1 tablespoon vinegar
Salt to taste

Preparation

Boil the potatoes with the carrots and water in a cooking pot for 15 minutes and drain. Boil the chicken in a cooking pot filled with water for 20 minutes. Shred the cooked chicken with a fork. Mix the shredded chicken, veggies, apple, and other ingredients in a bowl. Serve.

Chicken Salad

Preparation time: 10 minutes
Cook time: 10 minutes
Nutrition facts (per serving): 481 Cal (16g fat, 29g protein, 2g fiber)

The traditional chicken salad is here to add flavors to your dinner table, but this time with a mix of peas, chicken, and potato. You can try it as an effortless entrée with all sorts of bread.

Ingredients (6 servings)
2 carrots peeled and diced
1 russet potato peeled and diced
½ cup peas
1 stalk celery diced
4 cups cooked chicken shredded
1 cup mayonnaise
Juice of half a lemon
3 tablespoons of the brine from pickled jalapenos
Salt and black pepper, to taste
1 head or iceberg lettuce washed
Whole or sliced pickled jalapeños
Saltine crackers

Preparation
Add the potatoes and the carrots with water and ¼ teaspoon salt to a cooking pot and cook for 10 minutes on a simmer. Drain and transfer these ingredients to a bowl. Stir in the rest of the ingredients and mix well. Serve.

Venezuelan Salad (Salsa Carioca)

Preparation time: 10 minutes
Nutrition facts (per serving): 211 Cal (20g fat, 4g protein, 13g fiber)

This Venezuelan salad is the right fit to serve with all your Venezuelan entrees. The onion, tomato, and avocado are mixed with other veggies to make an amazing combination.

Ingredients (6 servings)
½ onion, chopped
1 tomato, chopped
1 medium avocado, pitted and diced
1 Serrano pepper, chopped
1 hardboiled egg, peeled and sliced

Dressing
1 tablespoon olive oil
1 tablespoon white vinegar
1 tablespoon hot pepper sauce
Salt and black pepper, to taste

Preparation
Toss the avocado, onion tomato, pepper, and egg on a platter. Mix the oil, vinegar, hot pepper sauce, black pepper, and salt in a bowl. Pour this dressing over the salad. Serve.

Tuna Salad

Preparation time: 10 minutes
Cook time: 20 minutes
Nutrition facts (per serving): 56 Cal (3.5g fat, 5.7g protein, 2g fiber)

This tuna salad is another most popular salad in this cuisine. Besides, it offers a superb taste from the mix of chickpeas, eggs, potatoes, and olives.

Ingredients (6 servings)
1 (15-oz.) can chickpeas, drained
1 ½ lb. potatoes, cut into pieces
4 hard-boiled eggs, quartered
½ red onion, diced
⅓ cup Kalamata olives in oil, drained
12 oz. of canned tuna
2 tablespoon olive oil
2 tablespoon red wine vinegar
Sea salt, to taste
Black pepper, to taste

Preparation
Boil the salted water in a large suitable pot and add potatoes. Cook until the potatoes are soft, drain, and then transfer to a bowl. Stir in the chickpeas, onion, olives, tuna, olive oil, vinegar, black pepper, salt, and eggs. Mix well and serve.

Potato And Beet Salad

Preparation time: 10 minutes
Cook time: 1 hour 20 minutes
Nutrition facts (per serving): 361 Cal (14g fat, 2g protein, 2g fiber)

Enjoy this Venezuelan potato and beet salad recipe with mixed flavors. This salad goes well with all other entrees.

Ingredients (6 servings)
2 lbs. of potatoes, cut into large bite-sized chunks
2 tablespoon olive oil
4 medium beets
1 large shallot, minced
½ cup frozen green peas cooked
½ cup frozen corn cooked
⅓ cup mayonnaise
1 teaspoon apple cider vinegar
1 teaspoon mustard
1 tablespoon fresh dill
Black pepper and salt to taste
½ cup queso fresco crumble

Preparation
Boil the diced potatoes in salted water in a saucepan for 20 minutes and drain. Toss the potatoes with 1 tablespoon oil in a bowl. Boil the beets in a cooking pan with boiling water for 60 minutes the drain. Peel and dice the beets into cubes. Toss the beet with 1 tablespoon of olive oil. Mix the

potatoes, beets, corn, green peas, and shallot in a bowl. Mix the rest of the ingredients in a bowl and stir in the veggie mixture. Mix well and serve.

Tomato Salad

Preparation time: 10 minutes
Nutrition facts (per serving): 179 Cal (16g fat, 5g protein, 3g fiber)

Tomato salad is a special fresh veggie salad, and it's a staple to serve with all the different entrees. Use this quick and simple recipe to get it ready in no time.

Ingredients (6 servings)
6 ripe tomatoes, diced
½ cup white onion, sliced
⅓ cup olive oil
¼ cup red wine vinegar
Black pepper and salt, to taste
1 handful parsley leaves, chopped
1 handful cilantro leaves, chopped

Preparation
Toss all the tomato salad ingredients in a salad bowl. Serve.

Hearts Of Palm Salad

Preparation time: 10 minutes
Nutrition facts (per serving): 339 Cal (23g fat, 20g protein, 6g fiber)

The classic hearts of palm salad is here to complete your Venezuelan menu. This meal can be served on all special occasions and memorable celebrations.

Ingredients (6 servings)
Salad
1 avocado, diced
2 tomatoes, diced
½ cucumber, diced
1 can of hearts of palm, diced
¼ cup cilantro chopped
Salt and black pepper, to taste

Mustard lime vinaigrette
¼ cup of fresh lime juice
½ cup of olive oil
1 teaspoon of sugar
1 teaspoon of Dijon mustard
1 pinch of black pepper and salt

Preparation
Toss the hearts of palm with the cilantro, cucumber, tomato, and avocado in a bowl. Mix the lime vinaigrette ingredients in a bowl and pour into the salad. Mix well and serve.

Venezuelan Tomato Slaw

Preparation time: 15 minutes
Nutrition facts (per serving): 93 Cal (7g fat, 1.4g protein, 4g fiber)

The Venezuelan tomato slaw is a delight to serve with all entrees. It's famous for its comforting effects, and the meal offers a very energizing combination of ingredients.

Ingredients (8 servings)
5 tomatoes, diced
½ English cucumber, quartered and sliced
1 red bell pepper, seeded and diced
½ cup onion, diced
½ cup fresh parsley, chopped
¼ cup lime juice
¼ cup olive oil
¼ cup green onions, diced
¼ cup fresh cilantro, chopped
2 tablespoons of cider vinegar
Salt and black pepper to taste

Preparation
Toss the tomatoes with the rest of the ingredients in a salad bowl. Serve.

Soups

Venezuelan Chicken Vegetable Soup

Preparation time: 10 minutes
Cook time: 1 hour 5 minutes
Nutrition facts (per serving): 310 Cal (11g fat, 22g protein, 6g fiber)

Make this Venezuelan chicken vegetable soup in no time and enjoy it with some garnish on top. Adding a drizzle of paprika on top makes it super tasty.

Ingredients (6 servings)

8 chicken thighs
4 garlic cloves, peeled
½ yellow onion, medium dice
3 medium-sized carrots, cut in ¼" rounds
2 ripe plantains, cut in ½" rounds
2 large leeks, cut in ¼" rounds
½ butternut squash, peeled, diced
2 sweet potatoes, diced
1 each yellow and red pepper, diced
3 bay leaves
1 bunch fresh cilantro
3 aji dulce, if available
2 ears sweet corn, cut into thirds
Black pepper and salt to taste
Fresh lime, to garnish

Preparation

Add the sweet potatoes and the rest of the ingredients, except for the lime and the corn. Cover and cook the soup for 1 hour on a simmer. Stir in the corn and cook for 5 minutes. Remove the chicken and discard the bones. Return the meat to the soup and garnish with cilantro and lime. Serve warm.

Quinoa Soup

Preparation time: 15 minutes
Cook time: 26 minutes
Nutrition facts (per serving): 453 Cal (15g fat, 6g protein, 0.7g fiber)

If you haven't tried the Venezuelan quinoa soup before, then here comes a simple and easy to cook recipe that you can achieve at home easily.

Ingredients (6 servings)
2 tablespoons cooking oil
2 cups yellow onion, diced
1 cup carrots, diced
1 poblano pepper, seeded and diced
3 tablespoons minced garlic
1 teaspoon dried oregano
2 medium red potatoes, diced
1 (15-ounce) can diced tomatoes
4 cups vegetable broth
2 cups of water
½ cup uncooked quinoa, rinsed
1 cup corn kernels
¾ cup diced zucchini
Salt and black pepper to taste
2 tablespoons chopped fresh cilantro

Preparation
Sauté the carrots, onion, and peppers with oil in a saucepan for 5 minutes. Stir in the oregano and garlic, then sauté for 1 minute. Add the broth,

water, tomatoes, and potatoes, and then cook it to a boil. Stir in the quinoa and cook for 10 minutes. Add the zucchini and corn, and then cook for 10 minutes on a simmer. Add black pepper, salt, and cilantro. Serve warm.

Minestrone Soup

Preparation time: 10 minutes
Cook time: 45 minutes
Nutrition facts (per serving): 488 Cal (17g fat, 27g protein, 2g fiber)

Try cooking the delicious minestrone soup with some unique combination of beans with stew meat at home to enjoy the best of the Venezuelan flavors.

Ingredients (6 servings)
1 tablespoon cooking oil
1 large onion, diced
1 tomato, peeled, seeded, and diced
2 large garlic cloves, minced
Salt and black pepper to taste
1-pound beef stew meat, cubed
10 cups water
½ (15.5 ounces) can garbanzo beans, drained and rinsed
½ cup of frozen corn
½ cup frozen lima beans
2 stalks celery, chopped
1 carrot, chopped
¼ cup cabbage, chopped
1 large potato, peeled and cubed
½ cup frozen peas
⅓ (16 ounces) box penne pasta
¾ cup crumbled cotija cheese
7 large fresh spinach leaves

4 leaves fresh basil

1 tablespoon water

Preparation

Sauté the tomato, onion, and garlic with oil in a cooking pot for 4 minutes. Add beef, salt, and black pepper. Sauté for 20 minutes. Stir in 10 cups water, garbanzo beans, lime beans, corn, celery, cabbage, and carrot. Cook for 10 minutes, and then add peas, pasta, and potatoes. Cook for 15 minutes. Blend the basil, spinach, cotija cheese, and 1 tablespoon water in a blender until smooth. Transfer this cheese mixture to the soup and cook for 4 minutes. Serve warm.

Black Bean Soup with Smoked Pork Chops

Preparation time: 10 minutes
Cook time: 8 hours 10 minutes
Nutrition facts (per serving): 276 Cal (17g fat, 7g protein, 3g fiber)

It's truly as if the Venezuelan menu is incomplete without a bowl of black bean soup with smoked pork chops. They're made with black beans, smoked pork chops, and sweet peppers.

Ingredients (8 servings)
1 lb. of dried black beans
8 cups of water or more if needed
1 tablespoon of salt
3 naturally hickory smoked pork chops, cubed
2 mini sweet peppers, cut into small cubes
2 tablespoon of corn oil
1 medium onion, chopped
4 garlic cloves
Cilantro

Preparation
Add the beans and water to a deep pan, soak for 4 hours, and then drain. Add the dried beans and 8 cups water to a slow cooker, cover, and cook for 8 hours on a Low setting. Blend the garlic, onion, and oil in a blender. Sauté the pork chops with oil in a skillet for 5 minutes per side. Transfer the pork chops to a plate lined with paper towel. Sauté the onion mixture in the same skillet for 3 minutes. Return the pork chops to the skillet and cook for 1 minute. Add the pork chops to the beans. Cover and cook for 30 minutes on a simmer. Remove the pork chop bones and garnish with cilantro. Serve warm.

Butternut Squash Leek Soup

Preparation time: 10 minutes
Cook time: 25 minutes
Nutrition facts (per serving): 155 Cal (8g fat, 3g protein, 2g fiber)

If you haven't tried this butternut squash and leek soup before, then here comes a simple and easy to cook recipe that you can recreate at home in no time with minimum efforts.

Ingredients (6 servings)
5 cups of water
1 chicken bouillon
1 lb. butter squash, peeled and cubed
½ an onion, split in half
3 leeks, washed and chopped
Salt and black pepper, to taste
2 cups of queso fresco cut into small cubes

Preparation
Boil the chicken bouillon and water in a large pot over medium high heat. Add the butternut squash, leek, and onion, cover, and cook for 25 minutes until soft. Blend the hot soup in a blender until smooth. Add black pepper and salt to season the soup. Serve warm.

Venezuelan Hen Chupe Soup

Preparation time: 15 minutes
Cook time: 28 minutes
Nutrition facts (per serving): 138 Cal (6g fat, 4g protein, 1.2g fiber)

The Venezuelan hen chupe soup is here to complete your Venezuelan menu. This meal can be served on all special occasions and celebrations.

Ingredients (8 servings)
8 cups chicken stock
1 cup onion, diced
2 garlic cloves, crushed
4 potatoes, peeled and diced
2 fresh corn cobs, peeled and sliced
1 can (15.25 oz.) whole kernel sweet corn
1 can (14.75 oz.) cream-style sweet corn
4 cups Cornish hen, cooked and chopped
¼ cup fresh cilantro leaves, chopped
Salt and black pepper, to taste
1 can (7.6 oz.) table cream
1 ½ cups queso fresco, cubed

Preparation
Add the chicken stock, garlic, and onion to a large pot then cook to a boil. Add the corn and the potatoes. Cover and cook for 15 minutes then remove. Add the corn to the water and cook for 10 minutes. Add the hen pieces and cilantro. Next, cook for 3 minutes. Adjust the seasoning with salt and stir in the cream. Garnish with cilantro and queso fresco. Serve warm.

Sancocho De Gallina

Preparation time: 10 minutes
Cook time: 25 minutes
Nutrition facts (per serving): 236 Cal (12g g fat, 5g protein, 3g fiber)

Here comes a delicious hen's stew! It's another special entrée on the Venezuelan menu. Cook it at home with these healthy ingredients and enjoy it.

Ingredients (8 servings)
1 large chicken, cut into pieces
1 lb. potatoes, peeled and diced
1 lb. cassava (or yuca), peeled and diced
¼ lb. pumpkin, peeled and diced
¼ lb. carrots, peeled and diced
6 corns on the cob, cut in half
1 large onion, chopped
1 leek, chopped
2 garlic cloves, chopped
Salt, to taste
1 teaspoon black pepper
Sofrito, to taste
Avocado, to garnish

Preparation
Add the chicken, water, salt, black pepper, leek, sofrito, garlic, and onion to a cooking pot. Boil and cook until the chicken is tender. Add the corn and the rest of the ingredients and cook for 5 minutes. Serve warm.

Mondongo Soup

Preparation time: 10 minutes
Cook time: 3 hours 25 minutes
Nutrition facts (per serving): 236 Cal (5g fat, 23g protein, 1g fiber)

You can serve this mondongo soup with warm tortillas and the famous Venezuelan salad. Pair the soup with white rice or warm bread.

Ingredients (6 servings)

1 lb. pork or beef honeycomb, bleached and clean
3 cilantro sprigs
1 teaspoon salt
¼ teaspoon pepper
8 cups water
2 limes, juiced
2 tablespoon oil
1 large red onion, chopped
1 teaspoon crushed garlic
½ cup chopped celery stalks
1 bell pepper, diced
6 plum tomatoes, diced
¼ teaspoon oregano
½ cup tomato sauce
3 potatoes, cubed
1 large carrot, diced
1 teaspoon agrio de naranja

Preparation

Add the honeycomb, ½ gallon water, ground pepper, 1 teaspoon salt, cilantro, and lime juice to a cooking pot and cook for 3 hours on a simmer. Remove the honeycomb from the liquid and cut into pieces. Sauté the garlic and the onion with oil in a pot over medium low heat until soft. Stir in the tomatoes, peppers, and celery and then cook for 2 minutes. Add the tomato sauce and the oregano. Stir in the potato, carrot, and honeycomb along with 3 cups water and cook for 15 minutes on a simmer. Serve warm.

Shrimp Meatballs Soup

Preparation time: 10 minutes
Cook time: 35 minutes
Nutrition facts (per serving): 401 Cal (14g fat, 29g protein, 3g fiber)

Let's have a rich and delicious combination of shrimp meatballs. Try with warm bread slices, and you'll simply love them!

Ingredients (6 servings)

1 ½ lbs. uncooked shrimp with shells on
6 cups water
Avocado oil
1 cup onion diced
4 garlic cloves minced
2 serrano peppers minced
1 red bell pepper diced
4 Roma tomatoes diced
1 cup celery sliced
1 ½ cups carrots sliced
1 small zucchini sliced
Handful fresh cilantro, chopped
1 jalapeño sliced in half
Salt and black pepper, to taste
⅓ cup masa harina
1 large egg
2 tablespoons tomato bouillon powder
½ teaspoon cumin seeds, crushed
½ teaspoon Mexican oregano, crushed

Preparation

Boil the shrimp with 6 cups water in a cooking pot for 4 minutes. Drain and grind the shrimp in a food processor. Sauté the onion, bell pepper, serrano pepper, and garlic with 1 tablespoon of oil in a skillet for 5 minutes. Remove from the heat and stir in the ground shrimp. Allow the shrimp to cool, add 1 egg, black pepper, salt, and masa harina, and then mix well. Make 20 meatballs from this mixture. Place these balls on a plate. Refrigerate these balls. Sauté the remaining onion, bell pepper, serrano, and garlic with 2 tablespoons of oil, a pinch black pepper, and salt, then sauté for 2 minutes.

Stir in the diced tomatoes, a pinch of salt, and black pepper and then cook for 6 minutes. Strain the broth and mix the bouillon. Stir in the carrots, celery, zucchini, ground spices, and shrimp meatballs and then cook to a simmer. Cook for 10 minutes then garnish. Serve warm.

Sausage Kale Soup

Preparation time: 15 minutes
Cook time: 65 minutes
Nutrition facts (per serving): 565 Cal (26g fat, 25g protein, 4g fiber)

If you haven't tried the sausage kale soup before, then here comes an authentic, simple, and easy to cook this recipe that you can recreate easily at home in minimum time.

Ingredients (6 servings)

12 oz. sausage, sliced
1 tablespoon olive oil
1 onion, diced
1 pinch salt
3 lbs. russet potatoes, peeled and sliced
2 teaspoons salt
2 quarts chicken broth
2 lbs. kale, chopped
1 pinch cayenne pepper

Preparation

Sauté the sausage with oil in a pot over medium-high heat for 5 minutes until brown. Transfer the sausage to a plate and add the onion and a pinch of salt to the same pot. Next, cook for 5 minutes. Stir in the potatoes, 2 teaspoons of salt, and chicken broth. Cook on a simmer for 10 minutes. Once soft, lightly mash the potatoes with a fork. Stir in the kale and sausage and cook on a simmer for 45 minutes.

Chicken Soup

Preparation time: 5 minutes
Cook time: 35 minutes
Nutrition facts (per serving): 159 Cal (7.1g fat, 17g protein, 1.8g fiber)

A warming bowl of chicken soup is all that you need to expand your menu. Simple and easy to make, this recipe is iconic.

Ingredients (6 servings)
1 bone-in chicken breast
1 onion, cut into wedges
4 sprigs fresh parsley
½ teaspoon lemon zest
1 sprig of fresh mint
6 cups chicken stock
⅓ cup noodles
2 tablespoon fresh mint leaves, chopped
Salt, to taste
¼ teaspoon white pepper

Preparation
Add the mint sprig, lemon zest, parsley, onion, chicken bread, and stock to a saucepan. Cook for 35 minutes and then remove the chicken from the pot. Slice the chicken into pieces. Strain the remaining broth and add to a saucepan. Add the chopped mint, pasta, white pepper, and salt. Cook until the pasta is soft. Stir in the chicken slices and the lemon juice. Garnish with lemon slices and mint leaf. Serve warm.

Bean Sausage Soup

Preparation time: 15 minutes
Cook time: 2 hours 10 minutes
Nutrition facts (per serving): 573 Cal (31g fat, 29g protein, 7g fiber)

A perfect mix of sausages, cabbage, macaroni, beans, and ham, this soup recipe is a warming bliss for all. Serve warm with your favorite bread.

Ingredients (6 servings)
2 lbs. spicy sausage, sliced
1-lb. ham hocks
1 onion, sliced
2 quarts of water
2 carrots, diced
3 potatoes, diced
1 small head cabbage, chopped
1 (8 oz.) can of tomato sauce
2 (15 oz.) cans of kidney beans
1 (16 oz.) package of macaroni

Preparation
Add the water, onion, ham hocks, and sausage to a large pot, cover, and cook for 1 hour on a simmer. Then remove the ham from the soup and cut it into pieces. Return the ham hock to the pot. Add the tomato sauce, cabbage, potatoes, and carrots, cover, and cook for 60 minutes. Add the pasta and the beans, cook for 10 minutes, and serve warm.

Chorizo Potato Stew

Preparation time: 15 minutes
Cook time: 40 minutes
Nutrition facts (per serving): 378 Cal (22g fat, 14g protein, 3.6g fiber)

Chicken potato stew is always served as a complete meal, and this one, in particular, is great to for a nutritious diet.

Ingredients (6 servings)
4 cups of water
1 (16 oz.) package of chorizo sausage, diced
2 potatoes, diced
½ head cabbage, chopped
3 carrots, diced
1 small onion, chopped
1 stalk celery, diced
1 (15 oz.) can of mixed vegetables, drained
2 tablespoons of parsley, chopped
½ teaspoon garlic powder
½ teaspoon celery salt
½ teaspoon ground red pepper
2 tablespoon cornstarch
2 tablespoons of water

Preparation
Add the chorizo, water, cabbage, potatoes, canned vegetables, onion, carrots, celery, parsley, celery salt, garlic powder, and red pepper to a large pot. Cook the mixture on a simmer for 40 minutes. Mix the cornstarch with water in a bowl, pour into the pot, and cook until the mixture thickens. Serve warm.

Pisca Andina

Preparation time: 15 minutes
Cook time: 20 minutes
Nutrition facts (per serving): 250 Cal (6g fat, 12g protein, 10g fiber)

The famous pisca Andina is essential on this Venezuelan menu. Try cooking them at home with these healthy ingredients and enjoy them.

Ingredients (6 servings)
10 cups chicken stock
2 cups cooked chicken, shredded
½ onion, chopped
2 garlic cloves minced
1 tablespoon olive oil
8 oz semi-hard cheese cubed
¼ cup cilantro, chopped
2 potatoes peeled and cubed
2 corns on the cob cut 3 pieces
3 cups milk
6 eggs
Fresh lemon juice to taste
Salt and black pepper, to taste

Preparation
Heat the oil in a suitable frying pan over medium heat. Sauté the onion until soft, add the garlic, and continue to cook for another 2-3 minutes. Combine the stock, potatoes, chicken, and corn in a suitable mixing bowl.

Allow the mixture to cook on a simmer until the potatoes are tender. It takes about 10-15 minutes. Combine the milk, cilantro, and cheese in a mixing bowl. Allow for another 2-3 minutes of simmering. Black pepper and salt should be tasted. Turn the heat off. The eggs should be cracked over the soup in different places of the stock pot so they don't contact. Cover the soup with a lid and let the eggs cook for almost 4-5 minutes more. Serve warm.

Main Dishes

Venezuelan Chocolate Chile Chicken

Preparation time: 15 minutes
Cook time: 25 minutes
Nutrition facts (per serving): 286 Cal (11g fat, 2g protein, 3g fiber)

This chocolate chile chicken is a must-have entrée that you can enjoy white rice and flatbread. Plus, with the help of this recipe, you can cook it in no time.

Ingredients (4 servings)
4 banana shallots, chopped
2 garlic cloves, chopped
1 tablespoon light olive oil
4 organic chicken thighs
4 organic chicken drumsticks
Juice and zest of 3 oranges
3 red chiles, diced
2 teaspoons dried mulato chiles
1 tablespoon coriander seeds
1 lb. canned chopped tomatoes
1 tablespoon dark muscovado sugar
4 oz. Venezuelan dark chocolate, broken into pieces
Bunch of coriander leaves

Preparation
Preheat the oven to 400 degrees Fahrenheit. Sauté the shallots and garlic in the olive oil in a casserole dish, add the chicken pieces, and brown on all sides. Simmer for 5 minutes with the orange juice and zest, fresh and dried

chiles, coriander seeds, tomatoes, and sugar. Cook for 20 minutes in the oven with the lid on. Remove the chicken from the oven, lift it out, and stir the chocolate into the leftover sauce. Serve with a substantial amount of chopped or torn coriander leaves poured over the chicken.

Beef And Black Bean Arepas

Preparation time: 10 minutes

Cook time: 25 minutes

Nutrition facts (per serving): 223 Cal (10g fat, 6g protein, 0.8g fiber)

These beef and black bean arepas will leave you spellbound due to their hot, saucy flavors and ground beefy filling.

Ingredients (6 servings)

3 cups masarepa

1 ⅓ lb. ground beef

2 onions

2 bell peppers

5 chiles

5 garlic cloves

1 tablespoon cumin

1 teaspoon chili powder

3 tablespoon chipotle hot sauce

1 can black beans

8 oz. queso Blanco

1 can diced tomato

Preparation

Mix the masarepa with water according to the package guidelines. Make thin, ⅓-inch-thick circles from the dough. Cook until browned on both sides in a dry cast iron skillet over medium/high heat. Making a pocket, split with a fork, leaving half of the edge intact. Cut the onions, peppers, garlic, and chilies in the meantime. If you don't want it to be as hot, remove the seeds from the chiles.

Drain the majority of the oil after browning the ground beef. Remove the pan from the heat and set it aside. In a small amount of oil, cook the onions and peppers. Salt. Add the garlic and chilies when they begin to brown. Stir in the cooked beef until it's evenly coated. After that, add the spices, tomatoes, and spicy sauce. Add the beans after rinsing them. Simmer for 15 minutes to ensure that all of the flavors are well combined. Fill the arepas halfway with the beef and bean mixture and then top with crumbled queso. Serve!

Venezuelan Meatballs Wrapped In Arepa Dough (Bollos Pelones)

Preparation time: 10 minutes
Cook time: 20 minutes
Nutrition facts (per serving): 185 Cal (12g fat, 6g protein, 0.4g fiber)

If you want something exotic on your menu, then nothing can taste better than these delicious homemade meatballs.

Ingredients (6 servings)
2 cups pre-cooked white cornmeal
2½ cups chicken broth
1 tablespoon vegetable oil

Ground beef filling
½ lb. ground beef
2 garlic cloves crushed
¼ cup paprika
½ white onion
3 strips bacon chopped
Adobo, to taste
½ teaspoon tomato paste
1 14-oz can tomatoes cut into small pieces
¼ cup green olives chopped
2 tablespoon capers
½ cup red cooking wine optional

Sauce

½ medium onion

½ red pepper

½ can tomatoes 14 oz.

2 tablespoon tomato paste

2 garlic cloves crushed

Salt to taste

Preparation

In a skillet, heat the vegetable oil and fry the crushed garlic, paprika, bacon, and onion for one minute. Add the ground beef and then the adobo sauce. When the meat is done, add the tomatoes, olives, capers, red wine, and tomato paste, reduce the heat, cover, and set aside to thicken the sauce. The chicken broth should be warm when making the dough. In a medium mixing basin, slowly whisk in the flour. Mix with a wooden spoon until the dough resembles cookie dough, then add one tablespoon of oil and knead for 3 to 5 minutes with your hands. Allow for a 5-minute rest period.

Combine the tinned tomatoes, paprika, and onion in a blender. Add the tomato paste, salt, and garlic to a sauce pan over medium heat. Cook until the sauce has thickened. Make a dough ball about the size of a golf ball, cut a hole in the center, fill it with ground beef, and close it with extra dough, making sure it stays spherical. Remove any excess dough and smooth over with a little water. Repeat with the remaining meat and dough until all of the ground beef is gone, and then lay them away until ready to cook. In a large pot, bring water to a boil. Carefully add the meatballs to avoid breaking them. Allow them to cook for about 12 minutes, or until they float to the top, indicating that they're done.

Carefully remove them from the pan, drain, and set aside for 5 minutes before serving. Place all of the pork balls on a serving plate and drizzle with sauce. Serve with white rice or on their own.

Venezuelan-Flared Pork Pernil

Preparation time: 15 minutes
Cook time: 4 hours 20 minutes
Nutrition facts (per serving): 228 Cal (6g fat, 4g protein, 3g fiber)

Venezuelan flared pork pernil is one good option to go for in the entrees. You can also keep them prep and cook ahead of time then reheat and serve whenever needed.

Ingredients (6 servings)
2 ½ lbs. pork shoulder, Boston butt, pernil
2 garlic cloves
1 small onion
1 bunch cilantro
1 jalapeño
1 cup orange juice
1 cup pineapple juice
1 lemon
Salt, to taste
Pepper, to taste
Ground cumin, to taste

Preparation
Rub the pork shoulder with salt and lemon after cleaning and cutting it. Place in a baking or roasting dish that's deep. Puree the garlic, onion, cilantro, jalapeno, orange and pineapple juices, and a teaspoon of cumin in a blender. Add salt and pepper to taste. Pour the marinade over the pork shoulder, wrap it in plastic wrap, and chill for a few hours or overnight.

Remove the pork from the fridge and set it aside to come to room temperature. Preheat the oven to 450 degrees Fahrenheit. Sear the sides of the pork shoulder in a big pan until they achieve a little color. Cook for 1 hour in a roasting pan covered in tin foil. Reduce the temperature to 400°F and continue to cook for another 3 hours, or until fork-tender. Cook uncovered for the last 20 minutes. On a serving plate, place the pork shoulder. Scrape any residual juices and drippings into a small saucepan. Strain the liquids, discard the solids, and reduce the liquids until thickened. Season to taste with black pepper and salt, as well as additional cumin, if needed. Serve with a tablespoon of gravy and cilantro springs on top.

Chicken With Rice

Preparation time: 10 minutes

Cook time: 40 minutes

Nutrition facts (per serving): 243 Cal (13g fat, 5g protein, 2g fiber)

Venezuelan chicken with Spanish style rice is mandatory on this menu.

Ingredients (6 servings)

4 tablespoon olive oil

1 cup onion, chopped

1 cup green pepper, chopped

1 cup red pepper, chopped

3 garlic cloves, chopped

¼ cup green onion, chopped

3 boneless chicken breasts, cut into small pieces

Salt and black pepper, to taste

1 ½ cup rice

3 cups chicken broth

1 teaspoon saffron

2 cups frozen mixed vegetables

Preparation

Sauté the green onion with garlic, peppers, onion, and 2 tablespoon of oil in a suitable skillet for 5 minutes. Rub the chicken with black pepper and salt. Push the onion mixture aside and sear the chicken for 5 minutes per side. Transfer the chicken and veggies to a plate. Sauté the rice with 1 tablespoon of oil in a deep skillet for 1 minute. Pour in the chicken broth, cooked chicken, saffron, and onion mixture. Next, mix well. Cook for 30 minutes on low heat until liquid is evaporated. Serve warm.

Venezuelan Chicken Sandwiches With Avocado

Preparation time: 15 minutes
Cook time: 45 minutes
Nutrition facts (per serving): 417 Cal (2g fat, 23 protein, 2g fiber)

Chicken sandwiches always taste great when served as an entrée or a side meal. These chicken sandwiches are a must due to their arepa bread and the stuffing.

Ingredients (4 servings)
12 oz. boneless chicken breast
1 ¼ cups arepa flour
½ teaspoon salt
1 ½ cups warm water
1 tablespoon canola oil
1 ripe avocado
¼ cup nonfat plain yogurt
Juice of 1 lime
⅛ teaspoon ground pepper
2 scallions, chopped

Preparation
At 350 degrees F, preheat your oven. Add the chicken and the cold water to a saucepan, cook on a simmer for 15 minutes, and then transfer the chicken to a plate. Mix the arepa flour and ¼ teaspoon salt in a medium bowl. Stir in 1 ½ cup warm water and mix to make a smooth dough. Knead this dough for 1 minute. Shape the dough into a ball, cover with a plastic

sheet and leave for 5 minutes. Divide the dough into 4 equal pieces and spread each into a 3 ½ inch round disc. Grease a suitable skillet with oil and place it over medium high heat. Sear each disc for 3 minutes per side. Bake the arepas for 15 minutes in the oven. Shred the chicken and transfer to a bowl. Mash the avocado in a bowl, add yogurt, chicken, salt, black pepper, scallions and lime juice, and then mix well. Slice each baked arepa in half, crosswise, to make a pocket. Divide the chicken salad into the arepas and serve.

Arepas With Black Beans, Mango, And Avocado

Preparation time: 10 minutes
Cook time: 25 minutes
Nutrition facts (per serving): 180 Cal (4g fat, 15g protein, 3g fiber)

These arepas stuffed with black bean and mango filling are everything I was looking for. The rich fillings make a complete package of taste and nutrients for a health enthusiast like me.

Ingredients (6 servings)
¼ cup 2 teaspoon vegetable oil
2 garlic cloves, chopped
1 (15-oz.) can black beans, rinsed and drained
1 chipotle chile in adobo sauce
Salt, to taste
1 small red onion, halved and sliced
Juice of 2 limes
2 cups white corn meal
½ cup fresh cilantro leaves
¼ crumbled Cotija cheese
1 small mango, sliced
1 avocado, halved and sliced

Preparation
Sauté the garlic with 2 teaspoon oil in a small saucepan for 1 minute. Stir in ½ teaspoon salt, ½ cup water, chipotle, and beans. Next, cook to a boil. Mix the onion with salt and lime juice in a bowl. At 350 degrees F, preheat your

oven. Mix 1 ½ teaspoon salt and 2 ½ cups warm water in a large bowl. Stir in cornmeal and mix well to make a moist dough. Divide the dough into 8 golf balls. Press each ball into a ½ inch thick patty. Set a skillet with ¼ cup oil over medium-low heat and sear the corn patties for 7 minutes per side. Transfer the patties to a baking sheet and bake for 10 minutes. Top the onions with cotija cheese and cilantro in a bowl. Divide the onion mixture into the corn arepas pocket and add avocado, beans, and mango slices. Serve.

Pabellón Criollo

Preparation time: 15 minutes
Cook time: 20 minutes
Nutrition facts (per serving): 295 Cal (17g fat, 28g protein, 3g fiber)

If trying Venezuelan cuisine for the first time, then the pabellon criollo is a must! It's served in a bowl with a mix of beans, pulled meat, and rice.

Ingredients (6 servings)
9 oz. rice
2 cups water
2 plantains
1 cup oil

Black beans
1 lb. black beans, canned
½ bell pepper, chopped
2 garlic cloves, chopped
1 onion, chopped
1 teaspoon black pepper
½ teaspoon cumin
2 teaspoons salt
3 ½ oz. sugar
3 ½ oz. bacon
2 tablespoons oil

Pulled meat
2 lbs. flank steak

13 cup water
1 bay leaf
1 small carrot
1 small celery
Oregano, to taste
Black pepper, to taste
½ bell pepper, chopped
2 garlic cloves, chopped
1 onion, chopped
1 tomato, chopped
1 teaspoon black pepper
½ teaspoon cumin
2 teaspoons salt
2 tablespoons oil

Preparation

Put the flank steak, water, bay leaf, carrot, celery, oregano, pepper, and salt in a large pot. Cook the beef until it's nice and soft (around 2 hours). Keep only 1 cup of the stock and discard the remainder. Chop the bacon, garlic, bell pepper, onion, and tomato in the meantime. Split the garlic, bell pepper, and onion in half. Just before the meat is done, start cooking the rice. Allow the meat to cool somewhat before cooking the beans with salt at the same time as you stir-fry the bacon with half of the garlic, onion, and bell pepper. Set aside a pinch of cumin and pepper. Shred the beef and stir-fry it with the remaining garlic cloves, bell pepper, and onion. Adds salt, cumin, and pepper to taste. Toss the beef with the chopped tomatoes and the saved stock. Bring to a boil, and then simmer for 10 minutes. While the bacon stir-fry is simmering, add the beans and cook them in the heated oil until the liquid has evaporated. Serve.

Holiday Ham Rolled Bread

Preparation time: 15 minutes
Cook time: 45 minutes
Nutrition facts (per serving): 139 Cal (0g fat, 8g protein, 2g fiber)

Do you want to enjoy a ham rolled bread with a Venezuelan twist? Then try this Venezuelan holiday bread recipe. You can serve it with your favorite bread on the side.

Ingredients (6 servings)
1 can of French bread loaf
6 oz. of ham slices
8 olives pitted
¼ cup of raisins
1 teaspoon of sugar
Flour, for dusting
1 egg yolk
1 teaspoon of panela

Preparation
Preheat your oven to 350 degrees Fahrenheit. Place the dough can on a floured surface and open it. Using your hands, roll it into a ball. Stretch the dough into a rectangle with the help of a rolling pin. Allow dough to rest for 5 minutes before attempting again if it shrinks too much. Inside the rectangle, place the ham slices side by side, leaving a little border of dough exposed. Make sure the olives, raisins, and sugar are evenly distributed throughout the ham. Make a tight log from the dough, making sure the seam is at the bottom. To keep the dough from inflating up, prick it all over

with a fork. Place the bread on a parchment paper-lined cookie sheet. Bake for 10 minutes, then whisk together the egg yolk and brown sugar. Brush the egg yolk mixture all over the surface of the bread when the 10 minutes are up. Cook for another 20 minutes, or until golden brown. Remove from the oven and set aside to cool.

Creamy Corn Souffle

Preparation time: 15 minutes
Cook time: 60 minutes
Nutrition facts (per serving): 570 Cal (46g fat, 12g protein, 2g fiber)

The Venezuelan cream souffle is an enriched entrée that you must serve at the winter dinner table. This recipe will add a lot of flavors, aroma, and color to your menu.

Ingredients (6 servings)
4 eggs
1 cup all-purpose flour
½ cup corn meal
2 teaspoon baking powder
3 tablespoon sugars
½ cup vegetable oil
1 teaspoon salt
2 cans of creamed corn
2 cans of corn

Preparation
At 350 degrees F, preheat your oven. Mix the flours with eggs, baking powder, sugar, and salt in a bowl. Stir in the corns and oil and mix well. Spread this mixture in a greased baking pan and then bake for 1 hour. Slice and serve.

Venezuelan Pasticho

Preparation time: 15 minutes
Cook time: 65 minutes
Nutrition facts (per serving): 226 Cal (24g fat, 4g protein, 1g fiber)

The famous pastiche is one of the Venezuelan specialties, and everyone must try this interesting combination of different toppings.

Ingredients (6 servings)
Bechamel Sauce
8 tablespoons butter
4 tablespoons flour
4 cups milk, warm
½ teaspoon salt
¼ teaspoon nutmeg
¼ teaspoon pepper

Pasticho
12 sheets of rolled flat lasagna pasta
8 cups Bolognese sauce
2 cups Parmesan cheese, grated
1 cup mozzarella cheese, shredded

Preparation
Sauté the flour with butter in a pan over medium heat for 2 minutes. Stir in the milk and mix until lump-free. Add the black pepper, nutmeg, and salt. Then cook for 5 minutes on a simmer. At 375 degrees F, preheat your oven. Layer a large baking sheet with a foil sheet. Grease a 13x9 inches

baking dish with butter. Spread ½ cup of bechamel sauce in the pan. Spread 3 pasta sheets over the sauce. Top these sheets with 2 cups of Bolognese sauce. Add 1 ½ cups of bechamel sauce on top. Drizzle ½ cup Parmesan cheese on top. Spread 3 layers of pasta sheet and repeat the layers of Bolognese sauce, béchamel sauce and Parmesan cheese. Cover the lasagna dish with foil sheet and bake for 50 minutes. Uncover and bake for another 15 minutes. Serve warm.

Venezuelan Asado Negro

Preparation time: 15 minutes
Cook time: 4 hours
Nutrition facts (per serving): 220 Cal (10.4g fat, 2.4g protein, 18g fiber)

Have you tried the famous asado negro? Well, here's a Venezuelan delight that adds round roast and carrots to your lunch in a delicious way.

Ingredients (6 servings)
4 lbs. eye of round roast
Salt and black pepper, to taste
6 garlic cloves, minced
⅓ cup Worcestershire sauce
⅓ cup vegetable oil
2 tablespoon granulated sugar
1 onion, diced
1 cup baby carrots
1 green bell pepper, seeded and diced
1 fresh oregano sprig
2 dried bay leaves
1 cup beef stock
1 beef bouillon
1 cup red wine
1 cup marsala wine
½ cup papelon, cut into small pieces

Preparation

Mix the beef with Worcestershire sauce, garlic, black pepper, and salt in a plastic bag. Mix well, seal, and refrigerate for 1 hour. Sauté the beef with oil and sugar in a deep pan until brown. Transfer this beef to a slow cooker. Stir in the onions, green pepper, and the rest of the ingredients. Cover and cook for 4 hours on High heat. Discard the bay leaves and oregano sprig. Slice the beef and return to the sauce. Serve warm.

Venezuelan Chicken Pot Pie (Polvorosa De Pollo)

Preparation time: 15 minutes
Cook time: 50 minutes
Nutrition facts (per serving): 211 Cal (17g fat, 6g protein, 0.7g fiber)

The chicken pot pie is the best way to enjoy soft and savory pie crust in the Venezuelan style. Serve with the freshly sautéed asparagus sticks.

Ingredients (6 servings)

2 tablespoon of olive oil
1 ½ cups onion chopped
1 cup of leeks, white part, chopped
¼ cup scallion the white part, chopped
3 garlic cloves minced
½ cup red bell pepper chopped
3 tablespoon jalapeño pepper, unseeded, chopped
2 chicken breasts, cooked and shredded
1 cup of white wine
½ cup of papelón
2 tablespoons of mustard
½ cup of Worcestershire sauce
2 bay leaves
2 cups of tomatoes chopped
½ cup raisins
¼ cup of manzanilla olives stuffed with red peppers, sliced
1 tablespoon of mini capers
4 tablespoon of tomato paste

Salt, to taste
Black pepper, to taste
2 pie dough crusts
1 egg for the egg wash
2 tablespoon of shredded papelón

Preparation

Sauté the onions, jalapeno, red bell pepper, scallions, leeks, and garlic with oil in a cast iron pot for 5 minutes. Stir in the capers, olives, raisins, tomatoes, bay leaves, mustard, papelon, wine, chicken, and Worcestershire sauce. Cook this mixture to a boil. Reduce its heat and cook for 1 hour. Remove the mixture from the heat and then add black pepper and salt. Cover and leave this stew overnight. Add the tomato paste and mix well. At 375 degrees F, preheat your oven. Place one pie crust in a pie dish and add the chicken stew. Cover the stew with the other pie crust. Cut a cross on top of the pie with a fork and brush the pie with the egg wash. Drizzle papelon on top and bake for 45 minutes. Slice and serve warm.

Carne Mechada

Preparation time: 15 minutes
Cook time: 50 minutes
Nutrition facts (per serving): 242 Cal (8g fat, 2g protein, 1g fiber)

If you haven't tried the Venezuelan carne mechada with black beans before, then here comes a simple and easy to cook recipe that you can prepare at home in no time with minimum efforts.

Ingredients (6 servings)
Carne Mechada
1 lb. beef
2 celery stalks, cut into 4 pieces
2 carrots, cut into 4 pieces
1 onion, quartered
1 onion, chopped
1 red pepper, diced
3 garlic cloves, crushed
Worcestershire sauce, to taste
1 teaspoon cumin
4 tablespoon tomato sauce
Olive oil, to taste
Salt, to taste
Black pepper, to taste

Black Beans
2 cups dry black beans, rinsed
3 oz. ham, diced

1 onion, diced

2 garlic cloves, crushed

1 bay leaf

Olive oil, to taste

Salt, to taste

Black pepper, to taste

Venezuelan white rice

1 cup white rice

2 cups water

½ teaspoon salt

1 teaspoon oil

1 garlic clove, crushed

½ onion, cut in half

½ green bell pepper, cut into strips

½ red bell pepper, cut into strips

Preparation

Boil the beef with carrots, quartered onion, celery, and water in a cook pot, cover, and cook for 4 hours on a simmer. Remove this mixture from the heat and allow it to cool. Remove the meat from the brine and shred it with a fork. Sauté the diced onions with 2 tablespoon oil in a suitable skillet until golden brown. Stir in the cumin, black pepper, salt, red bell pepper, and garlic and then sauté for 30 seconds. Stir in the beef and sauté until brown. Add Worcestershire sauce, tomato sauce, and a splash of water. Cook to a boil, reduce the heat, and cook for 15 minutes on a simmer. For the beans, sauté the ham and the onions with 4 tablespoons of oil in a pressure cooker for 5 minutes. Stir in the bay leaf and the garlic and then sauté for 1 minute. Add the beans, water, black pepper, and 1 tablespoon salt. Cover the pressure cooker and seal. Cook for 30 minutes on a high pressure. Once done, release the pressure completely and then remove the lid. For the rice, add the rice, bell pepper, onion, garlic, oil, and salt in a large pot. Sauté until golden brown then add water. Cover and cook the rice for 15 minutes. Serve the beef with rice and beans.

Short Crust Chicken Pie

Preparation time: 5 minutes
Cook time: 3 hours
Nutrition facts (per serving): 102 Cal (3g fat, 11g protein, 2g fiber)

This chicken pie is a typical Venezuelan entree, which is a must on this menu. It has this rich mix of saucy, shredded chicken.

Ingredients (6 servings)

Short crust

1 cup vegetable shortening
½ cup butter room temperature
¾ cup confectioner's sugar sifted
2 teaspoon salt
4 egg yolks
4 cups all-purpose flour
3-4 tablespoon water

Chicken Filling

4 cups shredded chicken
1 red pepper chopped
1 green pepper chopped
2 onions chopped
2 tomatoes chopped
2 garlic cloves chopped
¼ cup ketchup
1 tablespoon Worcestershire sauce
¼ cup red wine

2 cups chicken stock

¼ cup olives chopped

¼ cup capers

¼ cup raisins

1 tablespoon olive oil

Salt and black pepper, to taste

Preparation

Combine the flour, sugar, and salt in a mixing bowl using the mixer's paddle attachment. On medium speed, beat the shortening and butter together until smooth and creamy. One at a time, add the egg yolks, beating vigorously after each addition. Using a spatula, clean the bowl's sides. Add the flour mixture in a slow, steady stream until everything is well blended. If the mixture is crumbly and dry, add one tablespoon of water at a time until it's no longer crumbly. Separate the dough into two equal halves.

Refrigerate for at least 30 minutes after flattening the pieces into a disc. Heat the oil in a big pot over medium heat. Cook until the onions, peppers, and tomato are softened. Add black pepper and salt to taste. Mix in the chicken until everything is well mixed. Pour in the stock, wine, ketchup, and Worcestershire sauce. Cook, stirring constantly, until the wine has reduced by half. Combine the raisins, capers, and olives in a bowl. While rolling out the dough, allow the filling to cool.

Preheat your oven to 350 degrees Fahrenheit. A big baking pan should be greased. Between two sheets of parchment paper, roll out the bottom dough until it's ¼ inch thick. After taking off the top paper, invert the bottom paper into the baking pan. With your fingertips, press the dough into the pan's bottom and sides. Remove the paper, repair any breaks, and trim any excess dough. Using a fork, prick the bottom of the crust. 15

minutes in the oven Remove from the oven and set aside for 10-15 minutes to cool. Fill with the filling. Between two sheets of parchment paper, roll out the top dough until it's ¼ inch thick. Cook, stirring constantly, until the wine has reduced by half. Combine the raisins, capers, and olives in a bowl. While rolling out the dough, allow the filling to cool.

Venezuelan Shredded Beef

Preparation time: 5 minutes
Cook time: 25 minutes
Nutrition facts (per serving): 365 Cal (32g fat, 29g protein, 2g fiber)

Shredded beef is one of the traditional Venezuelan entrées that can be added to buns and bread slices to make a delicious burger or a tasty sandwich.

Ingredients (6 servings)
2 lbs. flank steak, cut into 4 pieces
2 garlic cloves minced
1 onion, chopped
1 red pepper sliced
3 tomatoes sliced
1 onion, 4 wedges
4 cups beef stock
2 teaspoon Worcestershire sauce
1 tablespoon tomato paste
1 teaspoon cumin
¼ cup ketchup
Salt and black pepper, to taste
1 tablespoon olive oil

Preparation
Add the beef, onion wedges, and stock to a pressure cooker. Cover and seal the lid. Cook for 20 minutes and then release the pressure completely. Remove the lid and keep 2 cups of stock aside. Shred the beef in a bowl

with a fork. Sauté the onion with oil in a deep pan for 5 minutes. Stir in the tomatoes, pepper, and shredded beef and then mix well. Stir in 1 ½ cups of stock, cumin, ketchup, tomato paste, and Worcestershire sauce. Mix well and adjust the seasoning with black pepper and salt. Serve warm.

Stuffed Turkey

Preparation time: 5 minutes
Cook time: 2 hours
Nutrition facts (per serving): 116 Cal (3g fat, 11g protein, 0.8g fiber)

You cannot imagine not having stuffed turkey on the dinner table for a festive occasion. So here's a delicious turkey recipe to sample.

Ingredients (6 servings)
Turkey
10 lbs turkey
1 bottle of wine
Salt and black pepper, to taste
Onion powder, to taste

Stuffing
3 large onions, peeled, chopped
6 plum tomatoes, chopped
2 red peppers, chopped
5 Granny Smith apples, cored and seeded
1 jar capers drained
2 cups raisins
1 cup green olives, pitted
6 strips of turkey bacon
4 eggs, beaten
2 teaspoon olive oil

Preparation

Inside and out, clean the turkey and pat it dry with paper towels. Place the turkey on a rack inside a roasting pan. Add the salt, pepper, and onion powder to taste. Cover and marinate for 2 hours in the fridge. Place the onions in a food processor and pulse a few times until finely chopped. Toss in the tomatoes and peppers and repeat the procedure. Cook the tomatoes, onions, and peppers in a large pan over medium heat with the olive oil until softened. Add black pepper and salt to taste. Meanwhile, pulse the apples in a food processor until sliced into small bits. Continue with the olives and the fried bacon in the same way. Place the sautéed onions, tomatoes, and peppers in a suitable mixing bowl. Combine the olives, bacon, apples, capers, and raisins in a mixing bowl. Mix until everything is well blended. In a separate bowl, whisk together the eggs. Tie the bird's legs together with a string and tuck the wings below it.

Preheat your oven to 325 degrees F. Make deep incisions all over the turkey using a thin knife. Stuff each incision with stuffing using your hands. Stuff the cavity and over the legs with the remaining stuffing. Season your turkey with black pepper and salt on the outside. Cover your turkey with cheesecloth that has been soaked. Preheat the oven to 350°F and place the roasting pan on the bottom rack. When a thermometer inserted into the meaty area of the turkey reaches 160°F, it's ready. Remove from the oven and set aside for at least 30 minutes, covered. The bird will be cooked until it reaches 165°F. Carve the meat and serve.

Balsamic Beef Roast

Preparation time: 10 minutes
Cook time: 4 hours
Nutrition facts (per serving): 232 Cal (10g fat, 28g protein, 6g fiber)

This balsamic beef roast will melt your heart away with its epic flavors. This roast is cooked with savory spices and delectable herbs on low heat for hours for a deep taste.

Ingredients (8 servings)
4 lbs. of eye round beef
12 oz. can of cola soda pop
½ cup of balsamic vinegar
2 leaves bay
1 ½ cups of beef stock
2 onions sliced
1 tablespoon of olive oil
Salt and black pepper, to taste
2 teaspoons of cornstarch
Chopped parsley, for garnish

Preparation
Using a paper towel, pat dry the meat and sprinkle all over with black pepper and salt. Heat the olive oil in a heavy-bottomed skillet over medium-high heat. Sear the beef on all sides, including the ends. When searing the steak, make sure it's practically black. Approximately 8-10 minutes Remove the steak from the heat and place it in the slow cooker. Meanwhile, add the onions to the same skillet and sauté until softened. Lift any meat bits from

the bottom of the pan with a wooden spoon. Add the stock, vinegar, and cola when the onions are tender. Bring the water to a boil. Place the bay leaves on top of the steak and pour the sauce over it. Cover and cook on high for 4 hours or low for 8 hours in a crock pot. Remove the steak from the pan and cut it into pieces. In a sauce pan, combine the sauce ingredients. Combine ¼ cup of the sauce and the cornstarch in a small bowl. Combine the ingredients and add to the remaining sauce. Toss in the sauce and bring to a boil. Pour the sauce over the beef. Enjoy.

Potato Cod Casserole

Preparation time: 10 minutes

Cook time: 35 minutes

Nutrition facts (per serving): 451 Cal (31g fat, 27g protein, 6g fiber)

Make this cod casserole in no time and enjoy it with some garnish on top. It has layers of cod, potatoes, and eggs, which make it super-rich.

Ingredients (6 servings)

2 lbs. dried salted codfish

4 Yukon Gold potatoes

3 tablespoon butter

2 yellow onions, sliced

2 garlic cloves, chopped

½ cup fresh parsley, chopped

¾ cup olive oil

1 ½ teaspoon red pepper flakes

Black pepper, to taste

4 hard-cooked eggs, chopped

10 pitted green olives

10 pitted black olives

Preparation

Soak the cod in salted water for 24 hours and then remove it from the water. Transfer the cod to a pan and pour in enough water to cover. Cook the cod for 5 minutes, then transfer to a plate. Add the potatoes and cook for 20 minutes until they are soft. Meanwhile, remove the cod skin and bones. Flake the cod in a bowl using a bowl. Mix black pepper, red pepper flakes,

1 tablespoon parsley, 1 garlic clove, and olive oil in a small bowl. Drain the potatoes and slice them. Sauté the onions with butter in a skillet until caramelized. Stir in the garlic and sauté for almost 1 minute. Place half of the onion slices in a greased 8x11 casserole dish, top them with half of the cod and half of the onion's mixture. Then repeat the layers with the remaining half of potato slices, cod, and onion. Bake the casserole for 15 minutes. Garnish with hard-cooked eggs, black and green olives, and parsley. Serve.

Mole Verde with Shredded Chicken

Preparation time: 15 minutes
Cook time: 40 minutes
Nutrition facts (per serving): 365 Cal (17g fat, 25g protein, 5.4g fiber)

It's about time to try some classic mole Verde on the menu and make it more diverse and flavorsome. Serve warm with your favorite herbs on top.

Ingredients (6 servings)
4 boneless chicken breasts
Water to cover chicken
Salt, to taste
1 cup raw pepitas
¼ cup sesame seeds
Avocado oil, to cook
1 medium onion chopped
5 garlic cloves sliced
6 serrano peppers sliced
6 tomatillos sliced in half
6 oz. fresh spinach washed
3 oz. fresh cilantro washed
1 teaspoon Mexican oregano
5 cups chicken broth or water
¼ cup chicken bouillon powder
¼ cup masa harina corn flour

Preparation

Add the chicken, water and salt to a cooking pot. Cover and seal the lid and cook for 35 minutes on a simmer. Remove the chicken from the broth and shred it. Return this chicken to the broth. Sauté the sesame seeds and pepitas with sesame oil in a skillet over medium heat for 5 minutes. Remove from the skillet. Sauté the garlic, tomatillos, serrano peppers, garlic, and onion with 3 tablespoons of oil in a deep pot for 8 minutes. Strain the broth and keep the chicken and broth reserved. Blend the sautéed vegetables, toasted seeds and 3 cups water in a blender. Add the oregano, masa harina, bouillon, cilantro, and spinach to a blender. Blend again until smooth. Pour in 2 cups of reserved broth and cook until warm. Fold in the shredded chicken. Serve warm.

Shrimp Ceviche

Preparation time: 15 minutes
Nutrition facts (per serving): 229 Cal (7g fat, 24g protein, 0.6g fiber)

Venezuelan shrimp ceviche is great to complete your menu, and this one, in particular, is great to have for a nutritious diet.

Ingredients (6 servings)
1 large garlic clove, chopped
½ tablespoon dried chile piquin, crushed
½ teaspoon Mexican oregano
4 large limes juiced
5 uncooked jumbo shrimp, peeled and deveined
4 peeled and deveined jumbo, cooked
¼ cup onion sliced
⅓ cup mini cucumbers sliced
Coarse sea salt, to taste
6 cherry tomatoes sliced
2 teaspoon Maggi seasoning
2 large radishes, sliced
½ tablespoon cilantro, chopped
Corn tostadas, chips or saltine crackers
Mexican style hot sauce
Lime wedges

Preparation
Mix the chile piquin with the garlic and the salt in a bowl. Stir in the lime juice and fold in the shrimp. Cover and refrigerate the shrimp for 20 minutes. Add the rest of the ingredients, mix well, cover, and refrigerate for 20 minutes. Serve.

Pork Sausage Tacos

Preparation time: 15 minutes
Cook time: 12 minutes
Nutrition facts (per serving): 338 Cal (10g fat, 33g protein, 3g fiber)

Now you can quickly make a flavorsome Venezuelan pork sausage taco at home and serve it as a fancy meal for you and your guest.

Ingredients (6 servings)

1 lb. pork longaniza
2 tablespoons Avocado oil
1 medium white onion, diced
3 large jalapeños sliced
Pinch of Mexican oregano
2 bay leaves
2 tablespoons white distilled vinegar
Salt and black pepper, to taste
8 large corn tortillas
Chopped cilantro

Preparation

Sauté the longaniza with the oil in a pan for 12 minutes and then transfer to a plate. Sauté the jalapenos and the onions with 2 tablespoons of oil, black pepper, and salt in a skillet for 5 minutes. Stir in the bay leaves, oregano, and vinegar and then sauté for 4 minutes. Add the longaniza and the pickled onion mixture on top of each tortilla and garnish with salsa and cilantro. Serve.

Venezuelan Pepito Sandwich

Preparation time: 10 minutes
Cook time: 3 minutes
Nutrition facts (per serving): 212 Cal (8g fat, 5g protein, 2g fiber)

Try making this delicious pepito sandwich with its unique combination of shredded vegetables, guasacaca and steaks at home for the best of the Venezuelan flavors!

Ingredients (4 servings)
4 hoagie-type bread rolls
2 (6-oz.) steaks
2 tablespoon vegetable oil
1 tablespoon minced garlic
2 tablespoon soy sauce
1 tablespoon Worcestershire sauce
Black pepper and salt, to taste
1 shredded vegetable like lettuce, cabbage and carrots, and tomatoes
Guasacaca, to serve

Preparation
Sauté the beef cubes with black pepper, salt, and 2 tablespoons of oil in a skillet until brown. Stir in the Worcestershire sauce, soy sauce, and garlic. Sauté for 3 minutes and then adjust the seasoning with the black pepper and the salt. Cut the rolls in half and stuff them with tomato, lettuce, and beef. Drizzle guasacaca on top and serve.

Venezuelan-Style Brisket

Preparation time: 10 minutes
Cook time: 3 hours 10 minutes
Nutrition facts (per serving): 280 Cal (4g fat, 23g protein, 0.5g fiber)

This Venezuelan style brisket makes a flavorsome serving with flatbread, so serve it at your dinner or as a delicious lunch.

Ingredients (10 servings)
5 lbs. whole trimmed brisket, cut into quarters
1 bunch parsley, chopped
1 bunch cilantro, chopped
2 large red onions, quartered
6 key limes, sliced
7 bay leaves
6 guajillo peppers, chopped
1 tablespoon dried oregano

Preparation
Rub the brisket liberally with black pepper and salt and then leave it for 1 hour. Place this brisket in a cooking pot and pour enough water to cover it. Add the oregano, guajillo peppers, bay leaves, limes, onions, cilantro, and parsley to the pot. Cook this mixture to a boil, cover, and cook on a simmer for 3-6 hours until the meat is tender. Shred the cooked meat and mix it with the salt, black pepper, lime juice, and cumin in a bowl. Serve warm.

Venezuelan Tamales (Hallacas)

Preparation time: 10 minutes
Cook time: 20 minutes
Nutrition facts (per serving): 394 Cal (19 g fat, 13g protein, 1g fiber)

Count on these tamales to make your dinner extra special and surprise your loved one with the ultimate flavors.

Ingredients (4 servings)

¼ cup 2 tablespoon olive oil
1 (8-oz.) boneless chicken breast half, chopped
6 oz. beef sirloin, chopped
6 oz. pork tenderloin, chopped
1½ cups chopped leek
1 cup chopped onion
⅓ cup chopped green onions
2 garlic cloves, minced
1⅔ cups chopped green bell pepper
½ cup chopped seeded Cubanelle chile
¾ cup chopped tomato
2½ cups chicken broth, divided
⅓ cup red wine vinegar
2 tablespoon brown sugar
1 teaspoon smoked paprika
½ teaspoon salt
½ teaspoon ground red pepper
¼ teaspoon black pepper
½ cup sliced shallots

½ cup sliced roasted red bell pepper
½ cup raisins
⅓ cup sliced pimiento-stuffed olives
½ cup chopped sweet pickles
½ cup small capers
½ cup sliced almonds
¼ cup chopped fresh cilantro
1 tablespoon annatto (achiote) seeds
1 ⅓ cups butternut squash puree
3 cups precooked white corn flour
½ teaspoon salt
16 (12-inch) squares of foil
3 hard-cooked large eggs, sliced
Reduced-fat sour cream, fresh cilantro leaves

Preparation

Over medium-high heat, heat a large nonstick skillet. Swirl 1 tablespoon of oil in the pan to coat it. Cook, stirring periodically for 5 minutes or until the chicken is done. Remove the pan from the heat. In a suitable skillet, heat 1 ½ tablespoon of oil; add the beef and pork and cook, stirring periodically, for 5 minutes or until done. Remove the pan from the heat. Reduce to medium-low heat and add 1 ½ teaspoon oil. Sauté for 5 minutes with the leek, onion, green onions, and garlic and then sauté for 5 minutes with the bell pepper and chile.

Cook for 5 minutes, or until the tomato has broken down. Using a wooden spoon, mash the potatoes. Place 1 cup of broth, vinegar, and the following 5 ingredients to the pot and brought to a boil over high heat. Return the meats to the pan, reduce the heat to medium-low, and cook for 30 minutes, or until the liquid has practically evaporated and the mixture has thickened somewhat. Remove from heat, allow it cool slightly, and then mix in the other 8 ingredients. In a small saucepan, combine ¼ cup oil and annatto seeds; simmer over low heat for 4 minutes, or until the oil is deep orange in color and the seeds are just beginning to brown. Remove from the heat and set aside for 10 minutes.

In a large glass measure, pour the remaining 1 ½ cups broth. Microwave for 1 to 2 minutes on HIGH, or until heated. Remove the annatto seeds and save 1 tablespoon of the annatto oil. Using a rubber spatula, scrape the remaining annatto oil into a food processor. Continue 2 minutes or until well combined and dough forms, add heated broth, squash puree, corn flour, and ½ teaspoon salt. Allow covered for 30 minutes in the food processor. With moistened hands, roll the dough into 16 (2-inch) balls and set on a cutting board lined with damp paper towels. Place 1 foil square on the work area, shiny side up, for each tamale; lightly brush annatto oil down the center of the square. Place 1 dough ball in the center of the square over the oil; with moist fingers, pat dough into a 6-inch circle.

Fill the dough circle with about ⅓ cup filling, leaving a ½-inch border. Add one egg slice on top. Fold the dough over the filling using the foil, top to bottom, then side to side, sealing the edges with moist fingers. Wrap the foil around the tamales from top to bottom and side to side to form a package. Steam the tamales for 1 to 1 ½ hours, covered, or until the dough is firm. Hallacas should be unwrapped. If preferred, top with sour cream and cilantro.

Caraotas Negras

Preparation time: 10 minutes
Cook time: 30 minutes
Nutrition facts (per serving): 281 Cal (14g fat, 22g protein, 1g fiber)

If you haven't tried the black beans before, then here comes a simple and easy to cook recipe that you can recreate at home in no time with minimum efforts.

Ingredients (4 servings)
1 ½ tablespoon canola oil
1 cup chopped onion
¾ cup chopped red bell pepper
1 teaspoon packed brown sugar
1 ½ teaspoon minced garlic
½ teaspoon fresh ground black pepper
1 teaspoon ground cumin
1 cup water
2 (15 oz.) cans black beans, undrained
1 teaspoon white wine vinegar

Preparation
In a suitable Dutch oven, heat the oil over medium heat. Cook, stirring periodically, for 5 minutes or until the onion and the bell pepper are soft. Cook for 1 minute, stirring constantly, after adding the sugar, garlic, black pepper, and cumin. Bring 1 cup of water and the beans to a boil. Simmer, partially covered, for almost 30 minutes or until slightly thickened, stirring frequently. Remove the pan from the heat and add the vinegar. Warm the dish before serving.

Chicken Dinner

Preparation time: 10 minutes
Cook time: 35 minutes
Nutrition facts (per serving): 441 Cal (21g fat, 33g protein, 3g fiber)

Best to serve at dinner, this chicken dinner can function as an energizing meal. It's a terrific Venezuelan version of delicious chicken pasta.

Ingredients (6 servings)
Chicken tenders
2 boneless chicken breasts
½ cup all-purpose flour
3 large eggs, beaten
1 ½ cups Italian breadcrumbs
⅔ cup peanut oil, for frying

Pasta
2 teaspoon salt
8 oz. rigatoni pasta
1 24-oz. jar marinara sauce
1 teaspoon Italian seasoning
½ teaspoon garlic powder

Casserole
2 cups mozzarella cheese, shredded
1 cup grated Parmesan cheese

Preparation

Using paper towels, pat dry the chicken breasts. Cut the dough into ½-inch strips, then cubes. To bread the chicken, create an assembly line by placing the four pieces in one shallow bowl, the beaten eggs in another, and the breadcrumbs in a third. The chicken pieces are breaded by coating them in flour, then eggs, and finally breadcrumbs. Place each on a platter lined with paper towels. Heat a quarter-inch of oil in a deep, heavy-duty frying pan or Dutch oven to 375 degrees F. Fry the chicken in batches, rotating once, for 3 to 4 minutes on each side. Drain the cooked chicken pieces on a dish covered in paper towels. Cut any larger nuggets into bite-size pieces once they've cooled. In the meantime, bring a saucepan filled with water to a boil and season with salt.

Cook the pasta according to the package directions, until not quite al dente. Drain thoroughly. Combine the marinara sauce, Italian seasoning, and garlic powder in a medium mixing bowl. Combine the noodles and the sauce in a mixing bowl. Remove the pan from the heat and set aside until the chicken is done. Preheat the oven to 375 degrees Fahrenheit. Start with a layer of spaghetti and sauce, then a layer of fried chicken, and finally 1 cup mozzarella. One more time, repeat these three layers. Bake for 25 minutes with the casserole covered in foil. Remove from the oven and sprinkle with Parmesan cheese, then bake for another 10 minutes, uncovered, until the cheese has melted. Serve.

Chicken with Potatoes

Preparation time: 10 minutes
Cook time: 35 minutes
Nutrition facts (per serving): 359 Cal (5 g fat, 33g protein, 1g fiber)

Count on this chicken with potatoes to make your dinner extra special and surprise your loved one with the ultimate flavors.

Ingredients (6 servings)
1 lb. Yukon Gold potatoes, cubed
7 tablespoon olive oil
Black pepper and salt, to taste
8 chicken thighs and drumsticks
3 Fresno chile peppers, chopped
2 garlic cloves, chopped
Grated zest and juice of 1 lemon
1 tablespoon 2 teaspoon red wine vinegar
1 teaspoon paprika
½ teaspoon honey
4 cups iceberg lettuce salad mix

Preparation
Toss the potatoes with 1 tablespoon oil, black pepper, and salt on a baking sheet and roast them for 10 minutes at 475 degrees F. Sear the chicken with oil, black pepper, and salt in a skillet for almost 6 minutes per side until golden brown. Blend 1 teaspoon salt, honey, paprika, 1 tablespoon vinegar, lemon juice, lemon zest, garlic, and chiles in a blender. Stir in ¼ cup olive oil and mix well. Place the chicken on the potatoes' baking sheet and pour

half of the sauce over the chicken and bake for 15 minutes. Toss the lettuce with black pepper, salt, 2 teaspoon vinegar, and 1 tablespoon olive oil in a bowl. Serve the chicken with the potatoes, the remaining chili sauce, and the lettuce mixture. Serve.

Venezuelan Pork Loin Chops

Preparation time: 15 minutes
Cook time: 17 minutes
Nutrition facts (per serving): 349 Cal (7g fat, 29g protein, 3g fiber)

If you want some new flavors in your meals, then these pork loin chops are best to bring variety to the menu.

Ingredients (6 servings)

Spice Rub

1 ½ tablespoon brown sugar
1 ½ teaspoon sea salt
½ teaspoon garlic powder
½ teaspoon onion powder
½ teaspoon paprika
¼ teaspoon freshly black pepper
¼ teaspoon dry mustard
¼ teaspoon fennel seeds, crushed
6 pork loin chops, boneless, ½ inch thick

Glaze

¼ cup maple syrup
2 tablespoon spicy brown mustard
1 pinch garlic powder
1 pinch paprika
1 pinch black pepper
1 pinch cayenne pepper
½ cup seasoned bread crumbs

1 tablespoon olive oil

1 tablespoon canola oil

1 garlic clove, crushed

Preparation

Mix all the pork spice rub ingredients in a bowl and rub over the pork loin chops. Cover and marinate the chops for 6 hours. Mix the breadcrumbs with oil and garlic in a bowl. Coat the pork loin with the breadcrumbs and sear for 6 minutes per side in a greased skillet. Pour the glaze over the pork loin. Cook for 5 minutes on a simmer and serve.

Pickle Meat Stew

Preparation time: 10 minutes
Cook time: 33 minutes
Nutrition facts (per serving): 470 Cal (12g fat, 24g protein,6 g fiber)

This meat stew recipe has unique pickle mixed flavors due to its rich blend of meat with veggies and pickles. Serve warm with rice or bread.

Ingredients (12 servings)
6 lbs. cooked beef chunks
3 tablespoon olive oil
2 large onions, chopped
8 medium tomatoes, chopped
1 (32-oz.) jar mixed pickles, chopped
Juice from meats
3 lbs. potatoes, peeled and quartered
18 eggs, hardboiled
6 tablespoon sugar
2 teaspoon powdered mustard
Vinegar from pickles
1 cup white wine
3 cups rice, cooked

Preparation
Sauté the onion with oil in a large pot until golden brown. Stir in the tomatoes and cook until their liquid is evaporated. Add the chopped meat and pickles and cook for 10 minutes. Stir in the water to cover the meat and potatoes and then cook for 20 minutes. Peel the boiled eggs, cut them in

half, remove the yolks from the whites, and mash the whites in a bowl. Mash the yolks with the mustard, sugar, and vinegar from the pickles in a bowl. Add this prepared mixture to the potatoes and cook for 5 minutes. Stir in the white wine and cook for 3 minutes. Serve the cooked meat with the mashed egg whites and rice. Serve.

Asado Negro Sloppy Joe

Preparation time: 15 minutes
Cook time: 3 hours 30 minutes
Nutrition facts (per serving): 316 Cal (21g fat, 5g protein, 0g fiber)

Are you in the mood to have some sloppy Joes on your menu? Well, you can serve this amazing recipe with avocado sauce.

Ingredients (8 servings)
4 lbs. eye of round roasts
⅓ cup vegetable oil
1 large white onion diced
6 garlic cloves minced
1 green bell pepper stemmed, seeded and diced
4 large tomatoes seeded, diced
¼ cup Worcestershire sauce
2 bay leaves dried
1 sprig oregano fresh
1 cup carrots diced
4 tablespoons salt
2 tablespoons sugar
6 hamburger buns toasted
4 tablespoons butter

Preparation
Remove any excess fat from the meat before preparing it. Combine the meat, Worcestershire sauce, garlic, salt, and pepper to taste in a resealable plastic bag. Refrigerate for at least one night. Remove the meat from the

plastic bag and pour the remaining marinade into a bowl when you're ready to cook the asado. Heat the oil in a big pan over medium-high heat. Add the sugar to the center of the pan once the oil has heated up. Allow it to dissolve without stirring and simmer until it turns brown. When it's hot enough, add the meat and sear both sides. Cook for another 15 minutes after adding the meat marinade. Continue to cook until the water comes to a boil. Cover for 10 minutes after it has done so. Adjust the heat to medium-low and add the carrots, green peppers, onions, bay leaf, oregano, beef bouillon, and beef stock. At this temperature, cook for 3 hours. Remove the meat from the slow cooker and place it in a blender with the remaining marinade and the vegetables. Purée until all of the ingredients are smooth in a sauce blender. Using a strainer, drain the sauce. Place the meat on a cutting board and cut into 12-inch pieces when ready to serve. Cook for 5 minutes in its own sauce from the blender over medium heat. Butter the hamburger buns and toast them in a pan over medium-low heat until golden brown, about 2-3 minutes. Both the meat and the sauce should be stuffed into the buns. Enjoy.

Steak With Onion and Tomato Sauce (Bistec A Caballo)

Preparation time: 10 minutes
Cook time: 20 minutes
Nutrition facts (per serving): 213 Cal (10g fat, 4g protein, 5g fiber)

Venezuelan steak with onion and tomato sauce is one delicious way to complete your Venezuelan entrée menu. So here's a recipe for a delicious meal.

Ingredients (6 servings)
Beef
2 lbs. beef sirloin divided into 4 portions
Black pepper and salt to taste

Sauce
2 tablespoon olive oil
1 medium white onion chopped
2 garlic cloves chopped
4 medium tomatoes chopped
1 teaspoon thyme
1 teaspoon dry oregano
½ teaspoon cumin
Salt and black pepper, to taste
4 fried eggs

Preparation

On both sides, season the steaks with Black pepper and salt. Preheat the grill for 5 minutes on medium high. Grill the steaks until golden brown, about 5-6 minutes per side, using a paper towel wet in a little oil to grease the grill. Set aside once cooked. You can also pan fried the steaks on your stove with around 2 tablespoons of oil over medium high heat for about 5-6 minutes per side. In a suitable skillet, heat the olive oil over medium heat. Cook, stirring occasionally, for about 3 minutes, or until the onion is transparent. Cook for another 1-2 minutes after adding the chopped garlic. Cook, stirring occasionally, for about 5 minutes, or until the tomatoes are soft. Add the thyme, oregano, cumin, black pepper, and salt to taste. Place the steaks on each plate, cover with the sauce, and finish with a fried egg. You can also serve this with white rice and avocado on the side.

Jamòn Crudo Con Palmitos

Preparation time: 15 minutes
Cook time: 25 minutes
Nutrition facts (per serving): 119 Cal (9g fat, 4g protein, 0.5g fiber)

The famous prosciutto wrapped palmitos with tostones are recipe is here to make your Venezuelan cuisine extra special. Serve them with ketchup.

Ingredients (8 servings)

¼ lb. Parma prosciutto
14 oz. hearts of palm
1 splash red wine vinegar
1 splash olive oil
3 sprigs fresh thyme
Black pepper, to taste
2 dashes Parmiggiano Reggiano

Tostones with Golf salsa

2 large green plantains, peeled and cut into 2-inch slices
⅔ cup vegetable oil
¼ teaspoon sea salt
2 egg yolks
¾ cup vegetable oil
½ lemon, juice
½ teaspoon salt
½ teaspoon Dijon mustard
2 tablespoons ketchup

Preparation

Combine the olive oil and the red wine vinegar in a mixing bowl. Crush the thyme sprigs and season with black pepper and salt to taste in the olive oil and red wine vinegar combination. Set aside while you prepare the palm heart. The can of palm heart should be opened and drained. If the palms are very huge, cut them in half. Roll one palm heart onto the end of an outstretched slice of prosciutto and cut in half. Repeat with the remaining prosciutto and palm heart. In a glass or plastic dish, arrange the prosciutto-wrapped palms and pour the olive oil and vinegar mixture over them. Allow at least 4 hours or up to one day to marinate. Serve on a good plate with plenty of fresh ground pepper and Parmesan cheese grated on top. Peel the plantain and cut it into 2 inch wide slices.

Heat a third of a cup of oil in a suitable skillet over medium-high heat. Once the oil is hot, cook the plantain slices for about 3 minutes, rotating once, just until tender. Plantains should be removed and drained on paper towels. Smash the plantains using a plantain press or a tin can to make them thinner. Allow the oil to return to its original temperature. Fry the plantain slices until golden brown on both sides, rotating occasionally. Remove the pan and absorb the excess oil with paper towels. Serve with a pinch of sea salt. Separate the egg whites from the yolks. Save the egg whites for another time and place the egg yolks in a medium bowl. On medium speed, whip the yolks with a hand mixer. In a thin steady stream, drizzle in the oil and continue to beat until the yolks and oil have emulsified. Combine the lemon juice and salt in a mixing bowl. Season with black pepper and salt to taste. Combine the mustard and the ketchup in a mixing bowl. Place in the refrigerator until ready to serve.

Stuffed Plantain Cups (Tostones Rellenos)

Preparation time: 15 minutes
Cook time: 17 minutes
Nutrition facts (per serving): 411 Cal (9g fat, 11g protein, 7g fiber)

When you can't think of anything to serve as the snack, then these delicious squares will help you to truly enjoy the authentic Venezuelan flavors.

Ingredients (6 servings)
3 cups canola oil for frying
1 green plantain
½ lb. cooked shredded beef
1 tablespoon mayo
1 tablespoon ketchup

Preparation
In a big pan, heat the canola oil. The plantains should be peeled and cut into fourths crosswise. They should be fried in hot oil until golden brown, about 5 minutes. Press the plantains flat with the bottom of a bottle, a small pan, to make a disc half their original size, then shape the disc into a little cup. Return the plantain cups to the hot oil and fry for another 5 to 7 minutes, or until golden and crisp. Remove the fish from the oil, drain on paper towels, and season with salt. Remove from the heat. Fill the plantain cups with the shredded beef and, mayonnaise and ketchup, if preferable. Serve right away.

Black Bean And Spice-Rubbed Torta

Preparation time: 10 minutes
Cook time: 10 minutes
Nutrition facts (per serving): 326 Cal (17g fat, 14g protein, 1.2g fiber)

Here's another classic recipe for your entrée collection. Serve the torta with a delicious hot sauce and enjoy the best of it.

Ingredients (6 servings)

1 12oz. container of firm tofu, sliced
1 can of black beans
1 tomato, sliced
1 avocado, sliced
8 oz. Monterrey Jack cheese, sliced
1 cup of lettuce, shredded
4 bolillos or French rolls
Salt, to taste

Tostones

2 ripe plantains, peeled and sliced
Oil, to taste
Salt or spice rub, to taste

Preparation

Combine the rub ingredients and apply on the tofu slices. Allow for at least 5 minutes of resting time. Heat the beans in a pot and mash them into a chunky paste once they're hot. Heat the oil in a skillet or sauté pan over medium heat. Place the tofu slices in a pan and brown on both sides for about 5 minutes. Meanwhile, toast the bolillos or French rolls in the oven or toaster oven until crisp and toasty. Slice the bolillo roll lengthwise and hollow out slightly to make place for the fillings. Spread the beans on the roll and sandwich the tofu and the cheese between the slices of bread. Return the roll to the oven to broil until the cheese has melted. Remove the torta from the oven and arrange the vegetables on top. Slice the ends off the plantains and cut a slit down the side of the plantain with a sharp knife, barely cutting deep enough to remove the peel. Plantains should be sliced into 12 inch medallions after gently removing the peel. Heat the oil in a sauté pan or cast iron skillet until it shimmers. Plantain medallions should be slipped into the oil and fried for 1-3 minutes on each side. Remove from the oven and place on a dish lined with paper towels. Flatten the plantains with a small plate or coffee cup until they are about 14 inches thick. Return the flattened plantains to the oil and cook for another 2 minutes on each side. Remove from the pan and place on a plate lined with paper towels. Serve.

Vegetarian Arepas

Preparation time: 10 minutes
Cook time: 25 minutes
Nutrition facts (per serving): 141 Cal (3g fat, 1g protein, 1.4g fiber)

Now you can enjoy arepas filled with avocado and plantains. They're entrée stuffed with delicious black beans.

Ingredients (6 servings)

2 cups masarepa (P.A.N. white corn meal)
2 ½ cups warm water
1 pinch of salt
Vegetable oil, for frying
1 can of black beans, rinsed
1 garlic clove, minced
2 teaspoon cumin
2 plantains, cut into rounds
Vegetable oil, to grease
1 ripe avocado, chopped
1 small onion, diced
1 jalapeño, seeded, cored, and diced
1 handful fresh cilantro, chopped
Juice of 1 lime
Salt and black pepper, to taste

Preparation

Mix the arepa ingredients until combined. Allow to sit for at least 15 minutes to incorporate. While the dough is resting, make the plantains, beans, and guacamole. Heat a very small layer of oil in a large pan over medium heat. Fry the plantains, sprinkling one side with a little salt, until golden brown on both sides. Drain on paper towels. Dump out all but a tiny bit of the frying oil. Mix in the beans, cumin, garlic, black pepper and salt, and heat through. Then remove the mixture from pan. Mash the guacamole ingredients together in a bowl and set aside. Alternatively, blend them together in a blender, substituting 2 tablespoon white vinegar for the lime juice, adding another handful of cilantros and 2 tablespoons of olive oil at the end. In the same large pan, heat the oil over medium heat. Scoop small handfuls of dough and pat them together to make ¼- to ½-inch thick discs that are free of cracks and creases. Fill the pan with as many as you can and cook until the bottoms begin to turn brown. Cook until golden brown and slightly springy to the touch on the opposite side. Fill with a scoop of black beans, a couple fried plantain strips, and a generous amount of sauce. Serve.

Arepas With Carnitas and Sweet Potato

Preparation time: 15 minutes
Cook time: 6 minutes
Nutrition facts (per serving): 456 Cal (15g fat, 6g protein, 0.7g fiber)

If you haven't tried these arepas stuffed with sweet potatoes, then here comes a simple and easy to cook recipe to replicate in no time with minimum efforts.

Ingredients (6 servings)
Arepas
2 cups precooked cornmeal
2 teaspoon salt
2 ½ cups warm water
Oil, for pan frying

Filling
Chipotle shredded chicken
Carnitas, to taste
Magic Green Sauce or other sauce, to taste
Black beans, to taste
Cotija cheese, to taste

Preparation
Combine the precooked cornmeal and salt in a mixing bowl. Remove any lumps with a whisk before adding the water and stirring until everything is well blended. Allow 5-10 minutes for the mixture to rest. Divide the dough into 8 pieces using your hands. Each piece should be rolled into a ball and

gently flattened to form a disc about 1 inch thick. In a suitable heavy skillet, heat a thin layer of oil (approximately ¼ inch deep) over medium heat. Fry for 6 minutes on both sides after adding the arepas. The arepas should have a dry, fried exterior that isn't too brown. Allow to drain and cool on paper towels. Fill the arepas by cutting them in half and stuffing them with the ingredients.

Patacón Hamburgers

Preparation time: 15 minutes
Cook time: 20 minutes
Nutrition facts (per serving): 635 Cal (38g fat, 10g protein, 2g fiber)

This new version of patacon hamburger is amazing, simple, and easy to cook. It's a hit for all the beef and plantain lovers.

Ingredients (6 servings)

2 green plantains
1 lb. ground beef
1 green tomato, sliced
4 cheese slices of choice
3 tablespoons of mayonnaise
3 tablespoons of ketchup
Drops of lemon juice
Salt and black pepper, to taste
½ cup of canola oil

Preparation

Make four hamburger patties by marinating the ground meat with your favorite seasonings. Grill or sauté until they're done to your liking. The cheese slices should be placed on top of the heated patties so that they melt with the heat. Peel the plantains before making the cones. Each one should be cut into three sections and fried in hot oil until two shades darker. Remove the plantains from the frying pan when almost done and flatten them with a plate or a rolling pin to about one quarter-inch thickness. Cook the plantains a second time in batches until crunchy on the outside but still delicate on the inside. To absorb excess oil, transfer to a plate lined with paper towels. While they're still hot, season them with salt. Place the patacón on a dish with a slice of green tomato on top, the hamburger patty with melted cheese, and then another patacón on top. Combine the mayonnaise, ketchup, and a few drops of lemon juice to make the fry sauce.

Desserts

Cannolo Siciliano

Preparation time: 5 minutes
Cook time: 10 minutes
Nutrition facts (per serving): 543 Cal (26g fat, 22g protein, 0.3g fiber)

Here's a special Venezuelan dessert role recipe, which is sensational to serve at special dinners and celebrations. Enjoy these creamy rolls with hot beverages.

Ingredients (6 servings)

2 ½ lbs. all-purpose flour
2 ½ whole eggs
2 oz. sugar
2 oz. vegetable shortening
1 pinch salt
1 pinch ground cinnamon
Marsala wine, to taste
Soybean oil, for deep-frying

Ricotta Cream

60 oz. ricotta cheese
20 oz. sugar
Liquid cream, to taste
1 teaspoon vanilla extract
2 drops cinnamon oil
1 oz. diced candied citron
1 oz. chocolate chips

Preparation

In a mixing dish, combine the flour, eggs, sugar shortening, salt, and cinnamon. Mix in the marsala until a stiff dough form. Divide the dough into two tablespoon-sized bits and roll each one into a 3-5-inch oval. Wrap each oval around a wooden stick and use an egg sealer to seal the dough. Leave them to rest for the night. Heat the oil in a deep fryer to 375 degrees F. Deep fry the dough shells for 10 minutes in heated oil until golden brown. Place the fried shells on a paper towel-lined dish. In a mixing dish, combine the ricotta cheese, sugar, cream, vanilla, citron, and cinnamon oil. Refrigerate for 1 hour after folding in the chocolate chunks. Using a small spoon, divide the filling among the fried shells. Serve.

Venezuelan Chocolate Marquesa

Preparation time: 10 minutes
Cook time: 10 minutes
Nutrition facts (per serving): 274 Cal (10g fat, 9g protein, 2.5g fiber)

Chocolate marequesa is one way to enrich your cravings with chocolate and milk. It has layers of creamy filling and milk soaked cookies.

Ingredients (6 servings)

2 cups unsalted butter, softened
¼ teaspoon salt
1 ½ cup sweetened condensed milk
1 ½ cup powdered sugar
¾ cup cocoa powder
½ cup milk
½ teaspoon pure vanilla extract
7 oz. Maria cookies
½ cup dark chocolate for drizzling, melted
1 ⅓ cups slivered almonds, crushed

Preparation

Blend the butter with salt in a bowl for 15 minutes on high speed until creamy. Slowly add condensed milk and beat for 2 minutes. Stir in the sugar and mix for 3 minutes. Add the chocolate powder and mix well for 2 minutes. Stir in 2 tablespoons of milk and vanilla and mix evenly. Layer a 9 inch springform pan with parchment paper. Spread ¼ of the chocolate cream in the pan. Soak the Maria cookies in the remaining milk in a bowl. Layer the cookies on top of the cream and repeat the layers of chocolate cream and cookies to get a total of 4 layers. Cover this suitable pan with a plastic wrap and refrigerate for 8 hours. Garnish with melted chocolate and almonds. Slice and serve

Quesillo (Venezuelan Flan)

Preparation time: 10 minutes
Cook time: 55 minutes
Nutrition facts (per serving): 270 Cal (3g fat, 11g protein, 2g fiber)

This Venezuelan flan is a special sweet and savory meal that you should definitely add to your menu.

Ingredients (6 servings)
1 cup white sugar
1 (14 oz.) can sweetened condensed milk
1 ¾ cups milk, or as needed
3 eggs
1 teaspoon vanilla extract

Preparation
At 350 degrees F, preheat your oven. Prepare a water bath in a large roasting pan. Melt the sugar in a saucepan by heating for 10 minutes over medium-low heat. Spread the melted sugar in a flan mold evenly. Add the condensed milk to a bowl and slowly pour in the vanilla extract and the eggs. Next, mix well until bubbly. Pour this milk mixture into the flan mold and cover it. Place this mold in the water and bake for 45 minutes. Remove the lid and bake for 15 minutes. Allow the quesillo to cool and then remove it from the pan. Slice and serve.

Pionono Relleno Con Dulce De Leche

Preparation time: 15 minutes
Cook time: 10 minutes
Nutrition facts (per serving): 419 Cal (14g fat, 19g protein, 7g fiber)

Forget cinnamon rolls; instead, try the relleno rolls with dulce de leche filling. They pair well with a hot beverage.

Ingredients (6 servings)
4 large eggs, separated
¾ cup granulated sugar
1 teaspoon vanilla extract
½ teaspoon almond extract
½ cup all-purpose flour
¼ cup almond flour
½ teaspoon salt
1 teaspoon baking powder
1 cup heavy whipping cream
2 tablespoons sugar
¾ cup dulce de leche
1 cup unshifted confectioners' sugar, for garnish
Caramel frosting, to taste

Preparation
Line an 11 x 17-inch jelly roll pan with waxed paper. At 350 degrees F, preheat your oven. Beat all the cake ingredients in a mixing bowl, except for the egg whites. Beat the egg whites in a bowl until foamy. Add the egg whites to the batter and mix evenly. Spread this batter in the pan and bake

for 10 minutes. Allow the cake to cool and then spread the sugar, caramel frosting, and dulce de leche on top. Roll the cake carefully then slice the roll. Serve.

Almond Ring Cake

Preparation time: 5 minutes
Cook time: 15 minutes
Nutrition facts (per serving): 376 Cal (14g fat, 22g protein, 18g fiber)

This Venezuelan almond cake will make your day with a delightful taste. Serve warm with your favorite salad on the side.

Ingredients (6 servings)

Cake

5 cups water
1 lb. almonds
1 lb. confectioners' sugar
3 egg whites
2 teaspoon almond extract
2 teaspoon potato starch flour

Frosting

4 cups confectioners' sugar
2 egg whites
1 teaspoon almond extract
1 teaspoon lemon juice

Preparation

Boil the almonds in hot water for 3 minutes, drain, and allow them to cool. Remove their skin and dry completely. Grind the almonds in a food processor to achieve a powder. Mix this almond flour with sugar in a bowl. Stir in the almond extract and the egg whites. Mix well to make a smooth dough. Cover it and refrigerate overnight. At 400 degrees F, preheat your oven. Roll the almond dough and divide into 8 portions. Roll each portion into a rope in descending order of length. The largest dough rope should be 18 inches long. Then continue decreasing 1-2 inches in each rope and shape them into rings by pinching the two ends together. Place the rings in a greased baking pan while adjusting their sizes to make a single layer of rings. Bake these rings for 15 minutes. Meanwhile, beat the frosting ingredients in a bowl and transfer to a pastry bag. Place the largest ring at the center, pipe the filing over it, and then continue adding rings and frosting on top in alternative layers. Serve.

Chocolate Mousse

Preparation time: 15 minutes
Cook time: 1 minute
Nutrition facts (per serving): 327 Cal (18g fat, 7g protein, 2.6g fiber)

This chocolate mousse has no parallel; this simple recipe has a delicious blend of dark chocolate, egg, and sugar.

Ingredients (4 servings)
½ cup granulated sugar
5 eggs
7 oz. dark chocolate
2 tablespoons margarine

Preparation
Add the chocolate chunks and butter to a bowl and melt by heating them in the microwave for 1 minute. Mix well until creamy. Beat the egg whites in a bowl until fluffy. Beat the egg yolks with the sugar in a mixer until creamy. Stir in the melted chocolate and mix well. Fold in the egg whites and mix. Divide the prepared mixture into the serving bowls and refrigerate for 4 hours. Garnish and serve.

Almond Cupcakes

Preparation time: 10 minutes
Cook time: 25 minutes
Nutrition facts (per serving): 141 Cal (4g fat, 2g protein, 1.1g fiber)

Here comes a dessert that's most loved by all. The almond cupcakes are not only served as a dessert, but also as a famous street food.

Ingredients (12 servings)

½ cup of water
2 egg yolks
3 eggs
2 oz. of almonds, chopped
1 cup of flour
¾ cup of sugar
1 cupcake baking sheet
¼ cup of almonds, chopped
1 tablespoon of powdered sugar
12 cupcake baking papers

Preparation

At 375 degrees F, preheat your oven. Mix the sugar with water in a suitable saucepan over medium heat and cook it to a boil. Beat the eggs, yolks, and 2 ozs. of almonds in a bowl. Add this prepared mixture to the saucepan and mix well until smooth. Divide this batter into a greased cupcake pan and bake for 25 minutes in the oven. Garnish with chopped almonds and powdered sugar. Serve.

Cornmeal Cake

Preparation time: 10 minutes
Cook time: 45 minutes
Nutrition facts (per serving): 567 Cal (26g fat, 29g protein, 1.2g fiber)

Try this cornmeal cake to serve all. Due to the cornmeal, coconut milk, and butter in the cookies, they achieve a great taste and good nutritional content.

Ingredients (4 servings)

1 tablespoon flour
1½ cups cornmeal
1 (13-oz.) can coconut milk
3 cups milk
2 cinnamon sticks
½ cup granulated sugar
3 tablespoon unsalted butter
½ teaspoon vanilla extract
½ teaspoon pumpkin spice
½ cup raisins
¼ teaspoon salt

Preparation

Pre-heat oven to 350 F. Mix raisins with a tablespoon flour and shake off excess. This will prevent the raisins from sinking to the bottom of the cake. Set aside. In a large, heavy-bottom pot, mix all ingredients, except the raisins and the vanilla. Whisk all together and cook over low heat until the mixture has thickened, stirring constantly. Fold in the vanilla extract and the raisins and remove from heat. Remove the cinnamon sticks and pour the mixture on the previously greased baking dish and bake uncovered for about 45 minutes to an hour, or until a knife comes out clean. Serve.

Coconut Cakes (Bolos de Coco)

Preparation time: 10 minutes
Cook time: 20 minutes
Nutrition facts (per serving): 624 Cal (40g fat, 10g protein, 2g fiber)

Coconut cakes are here to add flavors to your snack table; this effortless recipe gives you simple, tasty, and sweet coconut balls.

Ingredients (6 servings)

1 ¾ cups coconut, shredded
¾ cup white sugar
3 eggs
1 tablespoon lemon zest, grated

Preparation

At 350 degrees F, preheat your oven. Layer 3 muffin cups with paper cups. Mix the lemon zest, eggs, sugar, and coconut in a bowl. Divide the coconut mixture into the muffin cups. Bake them for 20 minutes in the oven. Serve.

Plantain Casserole

Preparation time: 5 minutes
Cook time: 50 minutes
Nutrition facts (per serving): 320 Cal (32g fat, 13g protein, 0g fiber)

Simple and easy to make, this recipe is a must on this menu. Venezuelan plantain casserole is a delight for the dinner table.

Ingredients (4 servings)

3 lbs. frozen plantains thawed

10 oz. semi-soft Latin white cheese grated

2 eggs

2 cans of condensed milk

2 tablespoons flour

1-2 tablespoon panela

Preparation

At 350 degrees F, preheat your oven. Cut the plantains in half. Mix the flour, eggs and condensed milk in a blender. Grease a 15x7 baking dish in cooking oil. Spread a layer of plantains in this dish. Add half of the panela, cheese, and milk mixture on top. Repeat the layers and bake for 50 minutes in the oven. Allow the casserole to cool and then slice and serve.

Dulce De Leche Sandwich Cookies

Preparation time: 15 minutes
Cook time: 15 minutes
Nutrition facts (per serving): 208 Cal (14g fat, 15g protein, 4g fiber)

The famous sandwich cookies are essential to try on the Venezuelan breakfast menu. Cook them at home with these healthy ingredients and enjoy.

Ingredients (6 servings)
Shortbread cookies
1¼ cup all-purpose flour
1¼ cup cornstarch
½ cup butter
1 teaspoon of baking powder
2 egg yolks
1 tablespoon lemon zest
3 tablespoons milk
1 teaspoon vanilla
½ cup powdered sugar

Filling and decoration
¾ cup dulce de leche
½ cup grated dry coconut
Powdered or icing sugar, to taste

Preparation

Mix the baking powder, cornstarch, and flour in a bowl. Stir in the lemon zest and the rest of the ingredients. Blend well with an electric mixture until all the ingredients come together as a cookie dough. Divide the dough into two balls and wrap each in a plastic wrap. Refrigerate the dough for 1 hour. At 375 degrees F, preheat your oven. Roll the dough portion on a floured surface into ¼ inch thick thin layer. Cut 2-inch rounds using a cookie cutter from the dough sheets. Place these cookies in a baking sheet lined with parchment paper. Bake the cookies for 15 minutes. Drizzle dulce de leche on top of the cookies and add coconut and sugar on top. Serve.

Venezuelan Polvorosas Cookies

Preparation time: 10 minutes
Cook time: 25 minutes
Nutrition facts (per serving): 172 Cal (5g fat, 1.4g protein, 2g fiber)

Venezuelan polvorosa cookies are another exceptional snack serving for the table.

Ingredients (8 servings)

1 cup vegetable shortening
1 cup granulated sugar
¼ teaspoon salt
1 teaspoon vanilla extract
½ teaspoon cinnamon
2 cups all-purpose flour
¼ cup powdered sugar for coating

Preparation

At 350 degrees F, preheat your oven. Layer two cookie sheets with parchment paper. Beat the shortening in a stand mixer for 2 minutes. Stir in the cinnamon, vanilla, salt, and sugar and then beat for 3 minutes. Stir in the flour and mix on a low speed. Roll the dough and divide the dough into 1 tablespoon sized balls. Place these balls on a baking sheet and press each ball into a cookie. Mark each cookie with a fork. Bake these cookies for 25 minutes in the oven. Drizzle sugar over the cookies and serve.

Drinks

Venezuelan Tizana

Preparation time: 10 minutes
Nutrition facts (per serving): 218 Cal (8g fat, 4g protein, 1g fiber)

This Venezuelan cocktail is famous for its blend of fresh fruit juices and pineapple chunks. You can prep this drink easily at home.

Ingredients (6 servings)

1 cup pineapple, diced
1 cup watermelon, diced
1 cup melon, diced
1 cup honeydew, diced
1 cup ripe mango, diced
2 cups strawberries, sliced
4 cups orange juice, chilled
4 cup mango juice, chilled
1 cup Grenadine or to taste

Preparation

In a pitcher, combine all of the diced fruit and the juices. To blend, stir everything together. Stir in the grenadine until it's mixed. Refrigerate for at least one hour overnight to allow all of the fruit flavors to blend. Allow it to cool before serving.

Chicha Venezolana

Preparation time: 5 minutes
Cook time: 40 minutes
Nutrition facts (per serving): 203 Cal (11g fat, 1g protein, 0g fiber)

The Venezuelan chicha is a festive rice drink to celebrate the winter holidays. Keep the drink ready in your refrigerator for quick serving.

Ingredients (6 servings)
1 cup rice
5 cups water
1 cinnamon stick
1 pinch of salt
2 cups whole milk
1 cup condensed milk
1 teaspoon vanilla essence
Crushed ice
Cinnamon powder, to taste

Preparation
Combine the rice, water, cinnamon stick, and a touch of salt in a medium saucepan. Bring to a boil, reduce to a low heat, and cook for 30-40 minutes, or until the rice is very soft. Remove from the heat and set aside to cool. Remove the cinnamon stick and discard it. Combine the rice mixture, whole milk, condensed milk, and vanilla essence in a vitamix or blender. Serve in a glass with crushed ice, a spray bottle of condensed milk, and a dusting of cinnamon powder.

Venezuelan Chocolate–Rum Drink

Preparation time: 5 minutes
Cook time: 15 minutes
Nutrition facts (per serving): 286 Cal (7g fat, 4g protein, 1g fiber)

Here's a special Venezuelan rum drink made from milk, cinnamon, and spices. Serve fresh for best taste.

Ingredients (4 servings)
½ gallon milk
3 whole star anise
2 sticks cinnamon
Zest of 1 orange
5 whole allspice berries
2 tablespoon brown sugar
½ lb. bittersweet chocolate
1 cup aged dark rum
Whipped cream

Preparation
In a suitable saucepan over medium heat, combine the milk, star anise, cinnamon sticks, orange zest, allspice berries, and brown sugar. Scald the milk and mix in the sugar until it dissolves. Cook for 10 minutes on low heat. Remove from the heat and allow it to steep for 10 minutes. Pour the contents of the strainer into a big pot. Heat until both the bittersweet chocolate and dark rum are melted and then remove from heat. Whisk vigorously for 5 minutes, or until the chocolate is completely dissolved. Serve with whipped cream on top.

Venezuelan Spiced Hot Chocolate

Preparation time: 5 minutes
Cook time: 25 minutes
Nutrition facts (per serving): 207 Cal (1g fat, 1g protein, 1.3g fiber)

Made with milk, orange zest, and spices, this beverage is a refreshing addition to the Venezuelan cocktail menu.

Ingredients (4 servings)
½ gallon milk
3 whole star anise
2 sticks cinnamon
1 orange, zested
5 allspice berries
2 tablespoon brown sugar
8 oz. semisweet chocolate, coarsely chopped
1 cup dark rum

Preparation
In a big heavy pot, combine the milk, spices, and sugar. Cook, stirring constantly to dissolve the sugar, until the milk barely begins to bubble around the edges over medium heat. Cook for 10 minutes on low heat. Remove from heat and steep for another 10 minutes before straining into another large heavy pot. Heat carefully before adding the chocolate and rum. Over a low temperature, whisk vigorously for 5 minutes, or until the chocolate is completely melted.

Guarapita

Preparation time: 10 minutes
Nutrition facts (per serving): 106 Cal (0g fat, 0g protein, 9g fiber)

This refreshing passion fruit drink is always a delight to serve at parties. Now you can make it easily at home by using the following simple ingredients.

Ingredients (8 servings)
3 cups rum
4 cups passion fruit juice
4 cups orange juice
1 ½ cup grenadine
8 whole limes
Mint leaves

Preparation
In a punch bowl, combine all of the ingredients with plenty of ice cubes. Garnish with mint leaves and serve in glasses with fresh ice cubes.

Piloncillo And Lime Drink

Preparation time: 15 minutes
Nutrition facts (per serving): 256 Cal (16g fat, 11g protein, 6g fiber)

The lime drink has no parallel in refreshment value. What's more, the best part is that all it requires is some mixture of the ingredients and it's ready to serve.

Ingredients (8 servings)
1 (8 oz.) piloncillo cone
4 cups very hot water
4 cups cold water
½ cup lime juice
Ice cubes

Preparation
Add the cone to a glass pitcher. Pour in 4 cups of hot water and mix well until the sugar is dissolved. Stir in lime juice, cold water, and ice cubes. Serve.

If you liked Venezuelan recipes, discover to how cook DELICIOUS recipes from **Balkan** countries!

Within these pages, you'll learn 35 authentic recipes from a Balkan cook. These aren't ordinary recipes you'd find on the Internet, but recipes that were closely guarded by our Balkan mothers and passed down from generation to generation.

Main Dishes, Appetizers, and Desserts included!

If you want to learn how to make Croatian green peas stew, and 32 other authentic Balkan recipes, then start with our book!

Only $2,99 at www.balkanfood.org/cook-books/

Maybe Hungarian cuisine?

Only $2,99 at www.balkanfood.org/cook-books/

If you're a **Mediterranean** dieter who wants to know the secrets of the Mediterranean diet, dieting, and cooking, then you're about to discover how to master cooking meals on a Mediterranean diet right now!

In fact, if you want to know how to make Mediterranean food, then this new e-book - "The 30-minute Mediterranean diet" - gives you the answers to many important questions and challenges every Mediterranean dieter faces, including:

- How can I succeed with a Mediterranean diet?
- What kind of recipes can I make?
- What are the key principles to this type of diet?
- What are the suggested weekly menus for this diet?
- Are there any cheat items I can make?

... and more!

If you're serious about cooking meals on a Mediterranean diet and you really want to know how to make Mediterranean food, then you need to grab a copy of "The 30-minute Mediterranean diet" right now.
Prepare **111 recipes with several ingredients in less than 30 minutes**!

Only $2,99 at www.balkanfood.org/cook-books/

What could be better than a home-cooked meal? Maybe only a **Greek** homemade meal.

Do not get discouraged if you have no Greek roots or friends. Now you can make a Greek food feast in your kitchen.

This ultimate Greek cookbook offers you 111 best dishes of this cuisine! From more famous gyros to more exotic *Kota Kapama* this cookbook keeps it easy and affordable.

All the ingredients necessary are wholesome and widely accessible. The author's picks are as flavorful as they are healthy. The dishes described in this cookbook are "what Greek mothers have made for decades."

Full of well-balanced and nutritious meals, this handy cookbook includes many vegan options. Discover a plethora of benefits of Mediterranean cuisine, and you may fall in love with cooking at home.

Inspired by a real food lover, this collection of delicious recipes will taste buds utterly satisfied.

Only $2,99 at www.balkanfood.org/cook-books/

Maybe some Swedish meatballs ?

Only $2,99 at www.balkanfood.org/cook-books/